THE ZODIAC KILLER

THE ZODIAC KILLER

The Story of America's Most Elusive Murderer

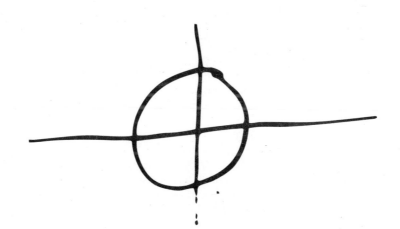

Michael Butterfield

ABOUT THE AUTHOR:

Michael Butterfield is a writer who has conducted extensive research into the Zodiac crimes for decades and served as a consultant for documentaries and director David Fincher's 2007 film, *Zodiac*. He was featured in the podcast *Monster: The Zodiac Killer* and appeared in the television shows Case: *Reopened*, *MysteryQuest*, *The Shocking Truth*, HLN's *Very Scary People*, *The Truth About Jim* on HBO Max, *History's Greatest Mysteries* with Laurence Fishburne, and *The UnXplained with William Shatner*.

This edition published in 2025 by Arcturus Publishing Limited
26/27 Bickels Yard, 151–153 Bermondsey Street,
London SE1 3HA

AD011078US

Printed in the UK

MIX
Paper | Supporting responsible forestry
FSC
www.fsc.org
FSC® C171272

Contents

Introduction

*"Where there is mystery, it is generally
suspected there must also be evil."*
Lord Byron

Modern monsters are often referred to as "serial killers," a popular term used to describe an individual who kills at least three victims with a hiatus or "cooling off" period between attacks. The label provided a ready-made description for infamous murderers such as Ted Bundy or the Green River Killer. These men were motivated by their hatred of the women they possessed and destroyed, a reality that made their horrific crimes somewhat easier to categorize and understand as we try to forget our primitive fears. Yet some monsters defy explanation and continue to haunt our collective nightmares long after they vanish without trace.

Unlike other notorious killers, the Zodiac had several different ways of operating. He was a phantom who shot and stabbed young couples, murdered a cab driver, and threatened to assassinate children on a school bus. He called police to report his crimes, left a handwritten message on a victim's car, and sent letters, greeting cards, bomb diagrams, and coded messages both to sow the seeds of confusion and to enhance his pleasure. He mocked his pursuers and teased them with clues as to his identity. The Zodiac wore a strange hooded costume decorated with his chosen symbol and he quoted from the Gilbert and Sullivan musical, *The Mikado*. He inspired countless villains in fiction, film, and television, and many hoaxers and copycat killers imitated his methods in real life.

Thousands of men were named as potential suspects and obsessed amateur sleuths accused members of their own families and others with books, websites, and documentaries. Despite the many theories and proposed solutions, the case remains unsolved. Like London's Jack the Ripper in Victorian times, the Zodiac has never been identified or captured. His legend was absorbed into pop culture and he became an American bogeyman.

More than fifty years after the brutal murders and taunting letters that shocked citizens of the San Francisco Bay Area, the Zodiac mystery is still one of the most terrifying and inexplicable stories in true crime history.

CHAPTER 1:
THE CRIMES

"I feel some nut is on the loose."
Lieutenant Colonel Verne Jensen

DECEMBER 20, 1968—LAKE HERMAN ROAD

Betty Lou Jensen was born in Hawkins, Kiowa County, Colorado on July 22, 1952. She later moved to Benicia, California, located in the North Bay of the San Francisco Bay Area. She lived with her sister and parents, was well liked, and active in her church youth group, the Prima Vera Council #32 of the Pythian Sunshine Girls. In her junior year at Hogan High School, Betty Lou was an honor student and had developed a talent as an artist. Unlike many other 16-year-old girls, Betty Lou had not dated boys, although she formed a platonic relationship with a teenager named Ricky. Her whole life changed in December 1968 when she met a young man during a church function at the Pythian Castle on Sonoma Boulevard.

David Arthur Faraday was born in San Rafael, California on October 2, 1951. He lived in Vallejo, California with his mother, sisters, and brothers. He attended Presbyterian church and was an Explorer and Eagle Scout who earned the highest honors. As a senior at Vallejo High School, David was a member of the wrestling team and active in school government. He was a good student and planned to become a teacher, but he skipped classes to drive Betty Lou Jensen home from school in his 1961 Rambler station wagon. Betty Lou's older sister, Melody, told her to bring David to meet their parents.

Ricky was reportedly upset when Betty Lou ended their relationship to be with David. A notebook found in Betty Lou's school locker included an entry about Ricky. "Do you know a kid named Richard [*last name redacted*]? I was going with him, until two days before the installation. He still phones me, and is threatening me to keep away from Dave. He said if he's ever close enough to Dave, he would punch him one in the teeth. I told him to leave me alone if he knows what's good [for] him." According to an unconfirmed account, David allegedly confronted Ricky at his school on Friday, December 20. There was no physical contact between the two boys and David walked away. Whatever may have happened, it didn't deter David from planning his first official date with Betty Lou later that night.

Betty Lou Jensen (left) and David Faraday (right).

David left his home around 7:10 p.m. and drove his sister to a meeting of the Rainbow Girls at the Pythian Castle. At 7:20, he returned home and his mother gave him $1.50 in change for the date. David left ten minutes later and arrived at the Jensen house where he was greeted by Betty Lou's father, Verne, and her mother, Virginia. Betty Lou wore a purple dress with a white collar and cuffs. David wore brown corduroy pants, a light-blue, long-sleeve shirt, and low-cut brown boots.

David and Betty Lou told Mr. and Mrs. Jensen they were going to a festival at Hogan High. David's sister, Debbie, later recalled him saying they were going out to Lake Herman Road to hang out with some other kids. The two teenagers promised to be home by 11:00 p.m. and climbed into the Rambler to begin their night together.

They arrived at the home of Betty Lou's best friend, Sharon, at 8:20. After a brief visit, the couple left at 9:00. According to some reports, the couple attended a Christmas concert at Hogan High and left sometime around 10:00. At 10:15, Helen Axe and her husband were driving through the rolling hills on the outskirts of Benicia along dark and secluded Lake Herman Road. They saw David's Rambler station wagon parked in a "lovers lane" spot in front of a gate at the entrance to the Benicia pumping station. A bright-yellow foreign car was also parked in the area. Helen said a man was sitting in the driver's seat, but she could not tell if the passenger was male or female. Shortly after 11:00, Peggie Your was with her husband Homer while he checked pipes and equipment as part of his job with the Frederickson Pipe Company. They noticed the Rambler parked with the front end pointed east, facing the large field to the left of the station entrance. A young girl in the passenger seat of the Rambler sat with her head on the shoulder of a boy in the driver's seat, who reacted to the passing headlights by placing his hands on the steering wheel. The Yours continued along the road and saw a red truck parked on nearby Marshall Ranch. Two men sat inside the truck, and one was holding a flashlight.

At roughly 11:20 p.m., Vallejo resident James Owen was driving along Lake Herman Road on his way to work the night shift at the Humble Oil company. He saw the Rambler parked outside the gated entrance and another vehicle was parked approximately 10 feet to the right of the station wagon. Owen was unable to describe the other car and he said he did not see anyone in or around the two vehicles. He continued along the road and said he heard what sounded like a gunshot when he was approximately one quarter of a mile away from the location.

Gruesome scene

Another vehicle soon approached. Benicia resident Stella Medeiros was on her way to pick up her 13-year-old daughter, and she was accompanied by her other daughter as well as her mother-in-law. They traveled along Lake Herman Road and the headlights suddenly revealed the Rambler station wagon parked near the pumping station entrance. The vehicle spotted by James Owen was gone. Stella could see the body of a young boy on the ground by the passenger side of the Rambler and the body of a young girl lying near the road. Stella immediately drove to Benicia and honked the car horn and flashed the headlights to attract the attention of a police patrol car. She stopped the car at the Enco gas station on 2nd Street, where Benicia police officer William Warner and Captain Danial Pita listened as Stella described the gruesome scene. Warner and Pita headed for the site of the incident, which they reached at approximately 11:28 p.m.

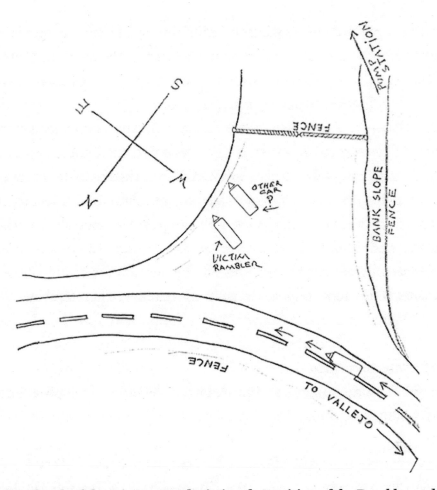

Police sketch of the crime scene depicting the position of the Rambler and the killer's car.

Captain Pita examined the body of Betty Lou Jensen. She was lying face down on the ground with several bullet holes in her back. Pita realized the young girl was dead. Officer Warner checked on David Faraday and noticed a bullet hole on the left-hand side of the victim's head. Warner believed he heard faint breathing and radioed for an ambulance in case the boy was still alive. Benicia police then notified the sheriff's office and the coroner.

Pita and Warner studied the crime scene. The passenger door of the Rambler was open, but the other three doors were locked. The passenger window was rolled down and the front seat was in a reclining position. Betty Lou's purse and white fur coat were on the back seat. Shell casings were found by the passenger side of the vehicle; one casing was on the floorboard, and one casing was found approximately 20 feet away. An apparent bullet hole in the rear window on the passenger side and another hole in the top of the station wagon indicated the killer fired those shots to force the victims out of the Rambler.

Other investigators arrived at the scene. Police Lieutenant George Little took photographs of the victims, the Rambler, and the evidence. Detective Sargent Pierre Bidou noted the hood of the Rambler was still warm. Solano County Sheriff's officers Butterbach and Waterman joined the group at 11:52 a.m. David Faraday was placed in an ambulance and transported to the local hospital. Betty Lou's body was covered with a blanket by the time *Fairfield Daily*

The Rambler station wagon at the crime scene on Lake Herman Road.

photographer Thomas Balmer arrived. His photograph of Betty Lou's shoes protruding from under the blanket appeared in the newspaper the next day. Coroner Dan Horan and Dr. Byron Sanford examined Betty Lou's body and pronounced her dead at 12:00 a.m.

Butterbach went to the hospital hoping Faraday might survive, but he was disappointed when informed that the teenager was dead on arrival at 12:05 a.m. He found 85 cents and Binaca breath drops in the boy's pockets. A class ring with a yellow setting and a red stone was held by the ring finger and middle finger of David's left hand, an indication that the ring might have slipped off his finger at the crime scene or in the ambulance. The bullet had torn the skin behind David's left ear, penetrated his skull, lodged inside, and caused a large bump on his left cheek. Dark discoloration around the wound was a burn created by the heat and gun powder residue from the barrel of a gun fired at close range.

Coroner Horan counted five gun-shot wounds on the right side of Betty Lou's back, extending from the area of the right shoulder down to near her waist. One bullet went through her upper back, exited through the right-hand side of her chest, penetrated her dress, and most likely disappeared into the hills surrounding the crime scene. Two bullets went into her lower back and exited from her lower abdomen, but one did not break through the dress and fell to the ground in the victim's path. Another bullet was caught in her undergarments. One bullet hole was found in the center of her dress at the front, along with the five other holes in the back. No gunpowder residue was found around any of the holes except the uppermost hole in the back, where a single grain of gunpowder was deposited after the weapon was fired several feet from the victim, although the grain may have been transferred by the bullet.

Coroner Horan and Sgt. Silva found nine Super X .22 cartridge casings at the scene. One bullet was recovered from the top of the Rambler and another was found in the floor mat on the left-side storage area of the Rambler station wagon. The bullets were Western copper-plated .22 long rifle rounds. Analysis determined that the bullets and cartridge casings corresponded to the .22 J.C. Higgins model 80 automatic rifle or perhaps a semiautomatic pistol. An inaccurate news report, which misidentified the murder weapon as a .32 caliber, led to speculation that two different weapons were used in the attack.

No escape

Detective Sargent Les Lundblad of the Solano County Sheriff's office consulted with Pita and Horan. They agreed the placement of the shell casings and other evidence indicated the killer fired shots into the Rambler to scare the victims and force them to exit the vehicle. The killer may have shot David first and then fired shots at Betty Lou as she tried to escape.

Family and friends of the victims were shocked by the seemingly senseless murders. No one could think of anyone who would want to hurt David and Betty Lou, but investigators quickly focused on possible suspects. The rejected suitor named Ricky was questioned, but he denied any involvement in the crime and said he was at his mother's home with others at the time of the shooting. Ricky's parents were separated, but his father, Donald, visited that night with his roommate, Mare Island Security Force Police Sgt. Leon Laughmiller. They watched a television show titled *A Global Affair* until Donald left sometime between 10:15 and 10:30 p.m. Sgt. Laughmiller said he left between 10:50 and 10:55. Ricky had no access to a car and he did not have enough time to get to Lake Herman Road without a vehicle. Ricky also had no way of knowing where the victims were at the time.

Ricky was confronted with the entries about him in Betty Lou's notebook. He denied threatening Betty Lou but admitted saying he would tell her parents that she smoked cigarettes. Ricky also stated he did not see David Faraday on December 20. Investigators concluded Ricky was not a viable suspect, but they did ask if he would submit to a polygraph test. At first, Ricky's father, Donald, reluctantly agreed to the test, but he later changed his mind because he did not believe his son could endure the stress because of a nervous condition. Donald noted the timeline of events demonstrated that Ricky could not have committed the crime and investigators would have to eliminate him as a suspect without the polygraph test.

Betty Lou's friend, Sharon, said a boy named Mark claimed David Faraday had some sort of altercation with a man who was described as a marijuana dealer. The incident reportedly occurred at the Vallejo Pancake House on Tennessee Street. According to Mark, David had discovered the man was "pushing grass" and intended to report him to police. The man allegedly threatened David, but no one seemed to know what was actually said during the incident. Another person later said the dealer may have been an employee where David worked. Some people speculated that David's alleged encounter with the dealer may have been linked to a marijuana bust on the night of the murders. Benicia police detective sergeant Pierre Bidou and Steve Armenta, a special agent with the Bureau of Narcotics, obtained a warrant and searched a small, city-owned structure near Lake Herman known as "the cottage." They confiscated approximately one and a half pounds of marijuana and then heard the police radio call about the shooting as they returned to the department with the evidence. Bidou later stated he did not believe there was any connection between the bust and David's reported encounter with the pot dealer.

A ranch hand named Benny Dow told investigators he was working near the crime scene during the day on Thursday, December 19, when he noticed a small foreign sports car parked on the side of the road. Dow thought the car was either cream or a white color. Two white males wearing sunglasses, aged 17 years old and 21 to 22 years old, were standing outside the car with a young female with long, straight, blond hair. Dow said the older man was holding a gun. Helen Axe said she saw a bright-yellow, foreign car on the side of the road shortly before the murders. The sighting of foreign cars and the man with the gun fueled speculation the unidentified trio was somehow involved in the crime.

Vallejo resident William Crow told police he was near the crime scene on the night of the murders and encountered a suspicious vehicle. Crow and his girlfriend were out for a drive in her sports car near the pumping station when he saw a blue car driving from Benicia towards Vallejo. The car passed Crow and then stopped in the middle of the road and backed up. Crow drove away but the other car followed at high speed. Crow steered his girlfriend's car towards the Benicia turnoff, but the other car continued straight ahead. Crow said the two people in the car were both Caucasians but he could not provide any further description. Years later, William Crow insisted there was only one person in the mysterious car.

Confusion grows

Another ranch hand named Bingo Wesher tended to sheep on property owned by Stella Medeiros, the woman who discovered the victims.

One hour before the shooting, Wesher said he saw a white Chevrolet Impala sedan parked by the south fence on the way to the pumping station. He also saw a red truck similar to the truck described by witnesses Peggie and Homer Your. Investigators identified the two men in the red truck as 29-year-old Robert Connley and his 69-year-old friend, Frank Gasser. They were hunting raccoons in the area and saw a vehicle pull into the entrance to the pumping station and stop next to the Rambler station wagon. Police realized the men had most likely seen the car driven by Homer Your. Connley and Gasser said they also saw a white, four-door 1959 or 1960 Chevrolet Impala in the area. The Yours said they saw a similar vehicle that night. Ballistics tests proved that the guns surrendered by Connley and Gasser were not used in the murders, and other weapons owned by other potential suspects were also eliminated.

A Vallejo police officer reported that a young boy and his friend were driving near the crime scene at 10:30 p.m. when they saw two vehicles on the Columbus Parkway, a hard-topped, two-door Oldsmobile and a 1963 blue Chevrolet Impala with two occupants inside. The cars turned from Lake Herman Road onto Columbus Parkway and headed toward nearby Blue Rock Springs Park. Several witnesses described a similar vehicle, but investigators were unable to identify the occupants.

The case remained unsolved despite the combined efforts of the Benicia Police Department, the Vallejo Police Department, the Napa Police Department, the Napa and Sonoma County Sheriff's Offices, and the Fairfield Police Department. Hogan High School student Jim Gaul and students from Vallejo High organized a committee to raise money for a reward for information which could help solve the case. The group hoped to raise $1,000 to fund the reward and a memorial art scholarship in Betty Lou's name. Debbie Baybado and Alice Daughtery held events and the students canvassed neighborhoods door to door, but they only raised a few hundred dollars.

David Faraday was buried at the Tulocay Cemetery in Napa, California. Betty Lou Jensen's body was placed in the Abbey Memorial Mausoleum. David's mother, Jean, told a reporter that the family was struggling with shock and grief in the aftermath of the murders. She worried that the killer would strike again and said, "He'll find it easier next time." Betty Lou's father, Verne, was also concerned and offered a warning which soon proved prophetic. "I feel some nut is on the loose."

JULY 4, 1969—BLUE ROCK SPRINGS PARK

Darlene Elizabeth Ferrin was born in Oakland, California on March 17, 1947. Her parents, Leo and Norma Suennen, raised Darlene with her sisters Linda, Pam, and Christine, along with their brother Leo. By November 1965, family problems caused Darlene to move away from home at the age of 18. She then met a man named James Phillips and the couple soon married in Reno, Nevada on January 1, 1966. The newlyweds traveled to the Virgin Islands and spent time in Albany, New York, where James briefly worked for the *Albany Times Union* newspaper.

Darlene and James returned to Vallejo in October 1966 and moved in with her parents. According to police reports, Mr. and Mrs. Suennen were upset when James remained unemployed, while Darlene worked as a waitress. They told James to find a job or move out immediately. He was hired as an assistant to the editor of the

Fairfield Daily Republic newspaper but was fired five days later for repeated absences. Once again, Darlene escaped from the situation by moving away. The couple lived in Pennsylvania and then returned to Vallejo several months later. Darlene took a job as a waitress at the Pancake House on Tennessee Street. She was popular with the customers and well liked by other employees.

Dean Ferrin was 23 years old and worked as a cook at the Pancake House. He was attracted to the young, free-spirited waitress nicknamed "Dee." He knew that she was having problems and wanted out of the marriage. Darlene moved back to Reno and filed for divorce. Dean drove up to see Darlene as their relationship turned into a romance. James moved to San Francisco and Darlene returned to Vallejo. Their marriage officially ended on June 2, 1967. Dean and Darlene married and rented an apartment at 506 Wallace Street. When Darlene discovered that she was pregnant, Mr. Suennen offered to help the couple make a down payment on a house at 1300 Virginia Street. Dean refinished the floors and painted the house as they worked together to make a home for their new baby girl.

By the summer of 1969, Dean worked as a cook at Caesar's Italian Restaurant, while Darlene waited tables at Terry's Restaurant. She became friends with waitress Bobbie Ramos, other employees, and even some customers, but Darlene also endured unwanted advances from a man who refused to take no for an answer. George was 23 years old, a neat dresser, approximately 150 lbs, 5ft 9in tall with black hair and an olive complexion. He worked as a bartender in Benicia and then trained to work at the Kaiser Steel plant, but he was laid off and found a job as an office manager in St. Helena near the vineyards of the Napa Valley. George met Darlene at Terry's in January 1969 and he later bought a truck from Dean. He was married but he repeatedly asked Darlene to go out with him. She refused and restaurant employees said he was very emotional when Darlene did not pay attention to him. Darlene reportedly told her friend Stephen Mageau that George had broken into her apartment and tried to rape her, but she convinced him to leave.

Stephen and his twin brother Michael Renault Mageau were born on October 29, 1949. They lived together until their parents divorced and then Stephen moved

Darlene Ferrin

to Los Angeles to live with their mother, Carmen, while Michael moved to Vallejo with their father, Robert. Michael had problems at school and was arrested in September 1968 for petty theft from a store on Springs Road. He teased Darlene that he was wanted by the FBI. He later said that he loved Darlene and wanted to marry her.

Lost girl

On the afternoon of July 4, 1969, Darlene finished her shift at Terry's and left around 4:00 p.m. She returned home and prepared to celebrate Independence Day with her husband. Darlene also tried to reach Michael Mageau by phone, but he was not home when she called. Shortly after 7:00, Dean's father, Arthur, arrived with Darlene's sister, Christine, and two young girls who would babysit while everyone else was gone. Darlene called Michael to tell him that she and Christine were going to the Miss Firecracker contest downtown and she would call him later. Darlene told the babysitters that she would be home around 10:00 p.m. and would then go to San Francisco, although she did not mention any reason for the trip. At some point, Darlene put on a blue, floral tank-top jumpsuit, although a police report mistakenly described the outfit as a "blue and white flowered slack dress." Around 7:45, Christine climbed into Darlene's Corvair and they drove off to attend events downtown and on Mare Island Channel.

At 9:00 p.m., Darlene called home and learned that a woman called for her at Terry's. She and Christina drove to Caesar's to see Dean around 10:30, and they decided to throw a party at their house after the restaurant closed. Darlene drove to Terry's, talked to Bobbie Ramos, and then took Christine home. She reportedly called Michael again and said that she would come over to get him soon. Back at the house on Virginia street, Darlene prepared for the guests. Dean's boss, Bill Leigh, called and asked her to get some firecrackers. Darlene told the babysitters that the plans had changed and then drove to Michael's house at 864 Beechwood Avenue. Michael later said they intended to get some food and were near Mr. Ed's diner when Darlene told him that she wanted to talk to him about something, so they took Springs Road to Blue Rock Springs Park, located on Columbus Parkway across the street from a large golf course.

Vallejo police officer Richard Hoffman was on motorcycle patrol when he passed by the parking lot of Blue Rock Springs Park after 11:40 p.m. He saw a blue sedan parked in the lot, but there were no other vehicles in the immediate vicinity and he continued his patrol. Sheriff's Deputy Ben Villareal later reported that he had driven by the lot shortly before midnight and saw a blue 1967 Ford sedan. Sometime after this sighting, the sedan left the lot and Darlene's

Corvair pulled into the parking lot near some eucalyptus trees. She shut off the ignition and headlights, but the radio continued to play. Rowdy partiers in three different vehicles entered the lot laughing and setting off firecrackers. Michael and Darlene watched the cars drive away and then noticed another vehicle that stopped directly behind them. The driver turned off the headlights and slowly pulled around to the left-hand side of the Corvair.

Michael was concerned and asked, "Do you know who that is?"

Darlene replied, "Oh, never mind."

All hell breaks loose

The other car then drove away along Columbus Parkway. Five minutes later, Michael watched as what appeared to be the same car reentered the lot and stopped approximately 10 feet behind the Corvair. The driver climbed out of the car with a bright light in his hand and walked toward Michael on the passenger side. Darlene and Michael believed the man was a police officer and they were prepared to produce their identification when the stranger pointed a gun directly at Michael and pulled the trigger. A bullet fractured Michael's jaw and sliced through his tongue. More bullets hit his right elbow, his right shoulder, and his neck. He desperately jumped into the back seat to escape, but another bullet hit his left thigh. Darlene was left exposed to gunfire and she was hit several times. The gunman then stopped, turned, and walked back to his car, but he reappeared after Michael cried out in pain. The man fired more shots into the Corvair and then climbed back into his car and drove away on Columbus Parkway toward Springs Road.

Michael struggled to get out of the car and managed to open the passenger door. He fell to the ground and remained there for some time until a Rambler station wagon entered the lot with three teenagers inside. Jerry, Roger, and Debbie had gone to the park in search of a girl Roger knew, but they were shocked to instead find Michael covered in blood. Jerry approached Michael and asked, "Are you all right?"

The wounds to Michael's jaw and tongue left him in agony as he tried to speak. "I'm shot, and the girl's shot. Get a doc."

The teenagers drove off to get help and they saw taillights in the distance as another vehicle turned onto Lake Herman Road. They went to Jerry's house and called the Vallejo Police Department after midnight. The call was answered by 26-year-old switchboard operator, Nancy Slover. She had planned to leave at 10:30 p.m., but decided to stay due to the large number of incoming calls that night. Her decision to stay secured her place in history and put her in the middle of a murder mystery. Nancy listened as the hysterical teenagers described the horrific scene at Blue Rock Springs Park, and she then directed officers to the park, hoping that the victims were still alive.

Officer Richard Hoffman arrived at the park and was soon joined by Officer Meyring. A late model gray Cadillac moved toward them. Meyring flashed the police lights and pulled the car over as Hoffman entered the parking lot. Michael Mageau was on his back near the back of the Corvair.

Hoffman asked, "What happened? Are you all right?"

Michael replied, "I've been shot."

Officer Meyring asked the teenage boy behind the wheel of the Cadillac for his driver's license. The boy complied and asked, "Is this about that guy laying down back there?" A teenage girl sat in the passenger seat, while Meyring identified the driver as a 19-year-old Vallejo resident named Andrew. [This individual had the same last name as another teenager named Gary, who gossip named as a possible suspect in the murders on Lake Herman Road.]

Officer Hoffman looked into the Corvair and found Darlene behind the steering wheel. He could see at least three bullet wounds on her right side. Blood was spattered around the interior of the car. Hoffman sent Officer Roy Conway to detain the driver of the Cadillac. Officer Doug Clark noticed that Darlene moved and apparently tried to say the words "my" or "I." He reached into the car and held Darlene's wrist. Her pulse was weak and she passed out.

Officer Conway walked over to Michael and asked, "Do you know who shot you?"

Michael said, "No."

"Can you describe this person?"

Michael could barely talk, so Conway asked some questions to obtain a description of the gunman as a white male in a brown car similar to Darlene's Corvair. Michael later described the man as a white male adult, short, possibly 5ft 8in, real heavy set, beefy build but not blubbery fat, possibly 195 to 200 lbs or maybe more, with a large face and short curly hair, light brown almost blond. The man wore a short-sleeved blue shirt.

"Did the man say anything?"

Michael answered, "No. He just, started shooting, and kept shooting."

One bullet was lodged in Michael's left leg, but other bullets had torn through him and gone on to wound Darlene. A total of nine entry wounds and seven exit wounds were later found on her body. Two bullets entered and exited Darlene's right arm and two more bullets entered and exited her left arm. She had five entrance wounds on the right side of her back and three of those bullets exited her body on the left side. One bullet was inside her chest near the second right rib and another was discovered near the third left rib. A bullet was lodged in the back of the driver's seat and another bullet was found in the door handle. Shell casings identified the ammunition as 9mm Luger rounds.

Detectives Ed Rust and John Lynch were in charge of the investigation and they consulted with the other officers on the scene. The ambulance arrived and Rust helped Michael onto the stretcher. He looked down and spotted a deformed bullet with a copper jacket. Rust checked on Darlene Ferrin and noticed that she was bleeding profusely but still breathing. Rust asked her what happened, but she could not speak and only moaned in pain. Darlene was placed in the ambulance and Officer Hoffman climbed in to ride with the victims to the Kaiser hospital. Rust examined the Corvair and he

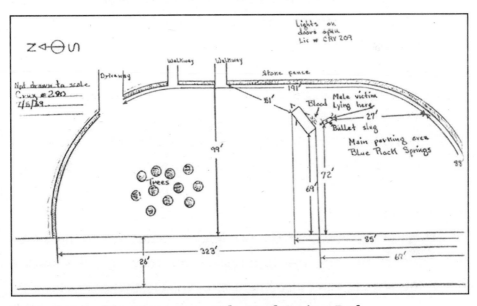

Police sketch of the crime scene at Blue Rock Springs Park.

saw another bullet on the driver's seat. Several brass shell casings were on the floorboard. The Corvair was towed to the Vallejo police garage.

The ambulance arrived at the hospital, but Darlene was pronounced dead on arrival at 12:38 a.m. Her body would be transported to the Twin Chapels funeral home and her blue tank-top jumpsuit and other clothing were placed in a police evidence locker. Nurses prepared Michael for the long surgery necessary to treat all of his gunshot wounds. Vallejo police officer Richard Hoffman took Michael's clothes as evidence and was surprised that the victim was wearing three pairs of pants, one T-shirt, three sweaters, and one long-sleeved shirt. The multiple layers of clothing seemed odd, but Michael may have worn the clothes to hide his thin physique.

When a stranger calls

At the Vallejo police department, switchboard operator Nancy Slover continued to cope with the aftermath of the shooting. She answered another incoming call at 12:40 a.m. and said, "Vallejo Police Department."

She heard the quiet but firm voice of a man. "I want to report a double murder."

Nancy replied, "Yes, sir, we have a report of gunshots." The man continued, but she interrupted to ask for his location. The caller ignored her and spoke in a monotone as if he was reading from a prepared statement.

"If you will go one mile east on Columbus Parkway to the public park, you will find the kids in a brown car. They were shot with a nine-millimeter Luger. I also killed those kids last year."

Nancy again tried to engage the man, but he ended the call with a long and theatrical "Goodbye." Nancy knew the man wanted to taunt and shock her with his words.

A Pacific Telephone company operator informed police that the call had been traced to a payphone at Joe's Union gas station on the corner of Tuolumne Street and Springs Road in Vallejo. The operator reportedly called the number, but someone answered and placed the receiver on the shelf in the phone booth. The caller was gone by the time officers Agenbroad and Peach arrived at the station in Unit 122. Officer Roy Conway joined them as identification technician Waricher dusted the phone booth and the receiver for fingerprints. Many people had undoubtedly touched the phone, but no fingerprints were found that could conceivably have been left by the caller.

Darlene's husband, Dean, and his boss, Bill Leigh, closed Caesar's restaurant and went to the house on Virginia Street. The babysitters later told police that Bill and Dean arrived sometime around 1:30 a.m. Dean was not surprised that Darlene was late and he drove the babysitters home before 2:00, but he was worried when he returned home and she was still not back. Bill reported answering the telephone while Dean was away, but no one was on the line. The phone rang again, but the caller did not speak. Dean's parents, Arthur and Mildred, told police that someone called their home at approximately 1:30 a.m. that night, but they could only hear breathing on the other end. Dean later came to the conclusion that the caller was a reporter or someone else who heard that a woman named Darlene Ferrin had been killed and then searched the phone book for her last name. According to some theories, the killer was responsible for the telephone calls.

Dean and Bill were surprised when police appeared at the front door. One officer said to Dean, "We need you down at the police station." Bill and Dean rode with the officers and learned that Darlene had been shot. They arrived at the Vallejo Police Department at 2:35 a.m. and Dean was then informed his wife was dead. He was overwhelmed but tried to answer questions about his movements and whereabouts that night. Bill confirmed Dean's account and took his friend home.

Michael Mageau survived the surgery and recovered at Kaiser hospital. Robert Mageau was stunned by the news that his son had been shot. He told police Darlene had called for Michael several times on Friday, but he did not know why they were together that night. Robert could not think of anyone who would want to harm Michael. Police hoped Michael would provide more information to help identify the killer. Days after the shooting, Vallejo police detective Ed Rust interviewed Michael at Kaiser hospital. Michael told Rust that he had no idea who would want to harm Darlene and he believed she would have told him if she had any problems with anyone.

Michael mentioned that the gunshots seemed somehow muffled, as if the killer had used a silencer on his weapon. George Bryant, 22, was the son of the caretaker at Blue Rock Springs and they lived in a small house in the park grounds. On the night of the murder, Bryant was in his bedroom approximately 800 feet from the crime scene. He heard firecrackers and then heard what sounded like a gunshot around midnight. Bryant emphasized that the sound of the gunshot was louder than the sound of the earlier firecrackers, a clear distinction between the two events and sounds. He heard another shot followed by a pause and then more rapid gunfire. Bryant also heard a car speed away. This account indicated the gunman did not use a silencer. The shots may have sounded muffled to Michael because he was inside the car and the first shot apparently hit him in the face at close range.

Detective Rust confirmed the basic details of Mageau's description of the killer as a white male adult, 26 to 30 years old, short, possibly 5ft 8in tall, with a beefy build, curly light brown/blondish hair, and a large face. Michael admitted he only caught a brief glimpse of the gunman's profile view as he walked away and he did not get a good look at the killer in the darkness. The interview left Rust doubtful as to whether Michael could identify the shooter.

Investigators interviewed many people in search of possible suspects, including Darlene's parents, her sisters Christina and Linda, the babysitters, Darlene's friends Bobbie, Evelyn, and others, the employees at Terry's, and more, but they could not identify anyone who would want to harm or kill Darlene. Linda told police that Darlene's closest friends were Bobbie Ramos and her cousin, Sue Ayers. She also said that a man named Lee brought her gifts from Tijuana. Dean Ferrin remembered the man in question as someone from New Zealand or Australia who Darlene once met on a bus from Reno. The man went on a trip to Mexico and brought Darlene a gift on his way back. Dean described the gift as a "some little trinket" and said he did not think Darlene ever saw the man again.

Linda, Bobbie, and others also remembered a man named George who repeatedly asked Darlene out on a date and became angry when she refused. George was a regular customer at the Kat Club where he reportedly bothered the female employees. One waitress reported that a customer claimed George said he killed Darlene. Subsequent investigation revealed the customer simply repeated an unsubstantiated story told by some members of Darlene's family.

When questioned at his home in Yountville, George denied any involvement in the murder and said he had not seen Darlene since May. He explained that he and his wife were home at the time of the murders. George's wife Judith corroborated his alibi. Police found no evidence linking George to the crime and he was cleared as a suspect.

Messenger of death

Investigators could not identify any viable suspects among those who knew Michael and Darlene, and the evidence seemed to indicate the killer selected the victims at random. The telephone call to the Vallejo police department after the shooting at Blue Rock Springs Park indicated the killer was responsible for that attack as well as the murders on Lake Herman Road in December 1968. Some investigators questioned whether the caller was actually involved in the crimes, while others believed a lone killer was on the loose and would soon strike again. The debate changed when three envelopes arrived at the offices of three Bay Area newspapers on July 31, 1969.

The San Francisco Chronicle, The San Francisco Examiner, and *The Vallejo-Times Herald* received messages from someone who claimed to be the killer. The sender had written "Please Rush to Editor" on the envelopes sent to the *Examiner* and the *Chronicle,* and two six-cent stamps featuring President Franklin D. Roosevelt were placed sideways on the upper right corners. The third envelope sent to the *Times-Herald* was similarly addressed but the four six-cent FDR stamps were sideways in the opposite direction. The sender included three virtually identical handwritten messages and three sheets of paper with carefully constructed blocks containing letters of the alphabet, astrological symbols, and other characters. The writer had used a blue felt tip pen to create a public confession to murder.

Dear Editor This is the murderer of the 2 teenagers last Christmass at Lake Herman & the girl on the 4th of July near the golf course in Vallejo To prove I killed them I shall state some facts which only I & the police know. Christmass 1 Brand name of ammo Super X 2 10 shots were fired 3 the boy was on his back with his feet to the car 4 the girl was on her right side feet to the west 4th July 1 girl was wearing patterned slacks 2 the boy was also shot in the knee 3 Brand name of ammo was Western Over [to next page] Here is part of a cipher the other 2 parts of this cipher are being mailed to the editors of The Vallejo time & SF Examiner. I want you to print this cipher on the frunt page of your paper. In this cipher is my identity. If you do not print this cipher by the afternoon of Fry. 1st of Aug 69, I will go on a kill ram- Page Fry. Night. I will cruse around all weekend killing lone people in the night then move on to kill again, untill I end up with a dozen people over the weekend.

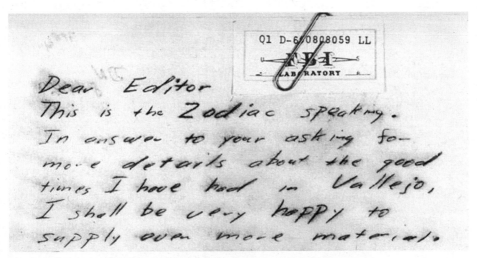

The beginning of the first letter to use the name "Zodiac."

Each letter was signed with a crossed-circle. The symbol is often used to depict a gunsight, a printer's registration mark, or a film leader, but the crossed-circle is also used to represent the Earth and the astrological Zodiac. In astrology, the crossed-circle represents the four seasons, the four points on a compass, and the houses of the Zodiac. The crossed-circle also serves as the basis for all astrological analysis and the creation of a horoscope for a birth chart. The name "Zodiac" and the crossed-circle only share a common meaning in astrology. The placement of the crossed-circle at the end of the letters could be interpreted as the signature "Zodiac."

J. E. Cirlot's 1971 book *A Dictionary of Symbols* states that the word 'zodiac' is derived from the Greek words *zoe* (life) and *diakos* (wheel) combined to form the word "zodiakos," meaning a circle of animals. *The American Heritage Dictionary* defines "Zodiac" as follows: "zodiac: n. 1.a. A band of the celestial sphere, extending about eight degrees to either side of the ecliptic (the sun's path), that represents the path of the principal planets, the moon and the sun. b. In astrology, this band divided into 12 equal parts called signs, each 30 degrees wide, bearing the name of a constellation for which it was originally named. 2. A diagram or figure representing the zodiac. (<Gk. zodion small represented figure). zodiacal, adj."

The Vallejo Times-Herald and *The Chronicle* published the text of the letters with the accompanying sections of the cipher, while *The Examiner* only published an article about the messages. Headlines about the writer's threat to kill again frightened citizens who were relieved when the weekend passed without further bloodshed.

The letters were written on Monarch-cut bond paper with the Eaton brand watermark. Some of the details included in the letters had been published in news reports, but the brand names of the ammunition used in the crimes were not public knowledge at the time. Anyone who had been at the crime scenes could have provided some of the details regarding the bodies of the victims, but most civilians did not have access. Vallejo Police Chief Jack E. Stiltz told reporters that he was not convinced the letter was written by the murderer and then said, "If it is the killer, we would like for him to write more facts to prove it."

The cipher was examined by cryptographers at the Central Intelligence Agency (CIA), Naval intelligence, the National Security Agency (NSA), and others. The killer's challenge inspired many amateur codebreakers who tried to solve the puzzle. In Salinas, California, a high school economics teacher and his wife studied the code for hours and tried to understand how the killer's personality might have influenced his creation of the cipher. Donald and Bettye Harden believed the killer's ego would compel him to use the word "I" and his need to boast of his crimes meant the hidden message most likely contained the word "kill." The couple searched for similar repeated patterns which could form doubled letters. Their strategy worked and revealed more clues about the mind of the murderer and his motives. The deciphered text of the message read:

I LIKE KILLING PEOPLE BECAUSE IT IS SO MUCH FUN IT IS MORE FUN THAN KILLING WILD GAME IN THE FOREST BECAUSE MAN IS THE MOST HONGERTUE ANIMAL OF ALL TO KILL SOMETHING ERYETHEYO A THRILLING EXPERIENCE IT IS EVEN BETTER THAN GETTING YOUR ROCKS OFF WITH A GIRL THE BEST PART OF IT IATHAE WHEN I DIE I WILL BE REBORN IN PARADICE AND ALL THE I HAVE KILLED WILL

BECOME MY SLAVES I WILL NOT GIVE YOU MY NAME
BECAUSE YOU WILL TRS TO SLOI DOWN OR ATOP MY
COLLECTING OF SLAVES FOR MY AFTERLIFE EBEO
RIET EMETH HPITI

The Harden's solution was published in the *Chronicle* newspaper and many readers developed their own theories about the cipher and its contents. The deciphered text did not reveal the killer's identity and the last 18 characters did not form coherent words in any language. Some people believed the remaining letters contained clues and the repetition of the letter E could indicate the killer's name was Foree or Forees. According to other interpretations, the 18 letters formed anagrams to read, "The tip I'm Robert E. EEEE," or "Before I meet them I pity them." According to one popular theory, the letters could be rearranged to read "Robert Emmet the hippie," a possible reference to the infamous Irish revolutionary, but the original text did not contain the duplicated letters R, P, and M necessary to complete the message.

A name for evil

Another letter arrived at the offices of *The Vallejo Times-Herald* on August 4, 1969, in response to the police request for more information about the crimes. Unlike the first set of letters, the new communication was written on Fifth Avenue brand paper manufactured by the Woolworth company. The three-page letter featured the same scrawled handwriting in blue ink.

Dear Editor This is the Zodiac speaking In answer to your asking for more details about the good times I have had in Vallejo. I shall be very happy to supply even more material. By the way, are the police haveing a good time with the code? If not, tell them to cheer up; when they do crack it they will have me. On the 4th of July: I did not open the car door. The window was rolled down all ready. The boy was origionaly sitting in the frunt seat when I began fireing. When I fired the first shot at his head, he leaped backwards at the same time thus spoiling my aim. He end-ed up on the back seat then the floor in back thrashing out very violently with his legs; thats how I shot him in the knee. I did not leave the cene of the killing with squealing tires & raceing engine as described in the Vallejo papers. I drove away quite slowly so as not to draw attention to my car. The man who told the police that my car was brown was a negro about 40 – 45 rather shabbly dressed. I was at this phone booth haveing some fun with the Vallejo cops when he was walking by. When I hung the phone up the dam XO thing began to ring & that drew his attention to me & my car. Last Christmass In the episode the police were wondering as to how I could shoot & hit my victoms in the dark. They did not openly state this, but implied this by saying it was a well lit night & I could see the silowets on the horizon. Bullshit that area is srowded by high hills & trees. What I did was tape a small pencel flash light to the barrel of my gun. If you notice, in the center of the beam of light if you aim it at a wall or celling you will see a black or darck spot in the center of the circle of light aprox 3 to 6 in. across. When taped to a gun barrel, the bullet will strike exactly in the center of the black dot in the light. All I had to do was spray them as if it was a water hose, there was no need to use the gun sights. I was not happy to see that I did not get frunt page cover- age.

The writer placed another crossed-circle at the bottom of the last page along with the words, "NO ADDRESS." News reports referred to the murderer as the "Code Killer" or the "Cipher Slayer," but the writer had chosen a name for himself and he would forever be known as "The Zodiac."

The Times-Herald editors delayed publication of the letter while investigators processed the evidence, but *The San Francisco Examiner* printed a photograph of the letter on August 4 with an article about the killer's message and his new name. Some statements indicated the "Zodiac" writer followed news reports and felt compelled to correct what he perceived as lies. An article distributed by The Associated Press and published in other newspapers stated that the "gunman opened a front door of the car and fired several shots with a semi-automatic pistol." The "Zodiac" writer responded with a denial, "I did not open the car door. The window was rolled down all ready." This account was confirmed by victim Michael Mageau. The writer also emphasized he did not speed away from the crime scene as reported by witness George Bryant.

Michael Mageau continued his recovery which included physical therapy and more surgery to repair the damage to his jaw, neck, left leg, and right arm. He sat in a wheelchair during a conversation with *Vallejo Times-Herald* reporter, Dave Peterson. Michael was the only person who had seen the killer, and he described the man as a white male, 25 to 30 years old, with a stocky build, approximately 160 lbs, 5ft 8in tall, with wavy or curly light-brown hair. According to Peterson's article, Michael "got his first good look at the slayer when he was walking away and was partly illuminated by his own headlights." Michael said, "He walked slowly and with his head down." Vallejo detectives Jack Mulanax and John Lynch had shown photographs of suspects to Michael, but he did not recognize anyone.

Michael recalled the events on the night of the murder and said the gunman did not speak before, during, or after the shooting. He stressed that his description of the onslaught was "not positive in his mind but was more impressional than exact." He pointed out that he was suffering from critical wounds during the ordeal. Michael eventually left the hospital to live with his father in Vallejo and later moved to San Pedro, but he was unable to escape the tragedy and memories of the terrifying attack.

Panic spreads

News coverage of the Zodiac's ongoing reign of terror frightened young couples who were afraid to park their cars in out-of-the-way spots at night. Police posted officers on stakeouts at some locations in the hope of catching the killer hunting for victims. People reported neighbors, coworkers, relatives, and others as possible suspects, and investigators were bombarded with tips that had to be checked out. Dozens of men were questioned, investigated, and eliminated from the growing list of suspects, while speculation raged regarding the killer's motives and possible connections to other crimes.

On August 3, the bodies of 15-year-old Kathie Reyne Snoozy and 14-year-old Debra Gaye Furlong were discovered on a hill in San Jose, California. According to medical examiner Dr. John E. Hauser, Kathie had been stabbed 150 times in her back and more than 50 times in her abdomen, chest, and neck. Hauser found at least 100 stab wounds on Debra's neck and the front and back of her body. There was no evidence of robbery or sexual assault. Speculation immediately linked the Zodiac to the Snoozy-Furlong murders despite the drastically different method of attack and the stunning overkill that resulted in hundreds of stab wounds left in the two victims. Hauser and Chief of San Jose Detectives Barton Collins believed that the lack of blood at the scene indicated the victims had been killed elsewhere and transported to the dumping location. The Zodiac did not move or transport his victims and he had not used a knife in his crimes. The Zodiac seemed like a possible suspect in the Snoozy-Furlong murders until police later arrested a man named Karl Francis Warner. He attended Oak Grove High School with the victims and was linked to the murder of another teenage girl who had been stabbed almost 40 times. Warner confessed and was sentenced to serve the rest of his life in prison.

In his first letters, the Zodiac threatened to kill more victims if three Bay Area newspapers did not publish the cipher, and that criminal act of extortion allowed the FBI to open a file on the case. The Bureau offered assistance with handwriting analysis, information about suspects, fingerprints comparisons, and more. The Vallejo police department, the Solano County Sheriff's Office, the Benicia police department, and other law enforcement agencies joined forces in the hunt for the Zodiac killer, but they found no viable suspects.

Investigators faced a new enemy, a bold and anonymous killer who was determined to be in the spotlight, and they were baffled when he fell silent after the last letter to the *Vallejo Times-Herald* in early August. The Zodiac's sudden absence led to wishful thinking that he had simply disappeared and the threat was gone, but the killer carefully planned his next attack and soon returned to commit a crime more shocking than anyone could have imagined.

SEPTEMBER 27, 1969—LAKE BERRYESSA

Cecelia Ann Shepard was born in Andhra Pradesh, India, on January 1, 1947. She was raised by her parents Wilma and Robert and grew up with her sisters Kathy and Carolyn. She graduated from the Seventh-day Adventist [a Protestant Christian denomination] San Gabriel Academy in 1965 and then attended the La Sierra campus of Loma Linda University in 1966 and 1967. Cecelia transferred to Pacific Union College in Angwin, California, located approximately 40 miles from Vallejo. She met Judy and they quickly became best friends. Cecelia also had a brief romance with a PUC student named Bryan Hartnell. The relationship ended when she decided to continue her music studies at the University of California in Riverside for her junior year. Bryan and Cecelia remained friends after she moved away, and she returned for a visit to the PUC campus on September 27, 1969.

Bryan Calvin Hartnell was born on July 1, 1949 in Wala Wala, Washington. He was tall, handsome, and a member of the Seventh-day Adventist Church. He was happy to reunite with Cecelia and they decided to spend the day together with Judy. They left the PUC campus in Angwin at approximately 1:00 p.m. and headed south in Bryan's white Volkswagen Karmann Ghia.

The trio stopped at a rummage sale in St. Helena and Bryan bought a used television set for his room. He soon realized the set was too big to fit in the small Karmann Ghia with the two girls, so Bryan drove back to the PUC campus, dropped off the TV, and then went back to the rummage sale. Judy decided to stay in St. Helena and Bryan and Cecelia mentioned they were going to San Francisco. Judy said her goodbyes and the couple left together.

 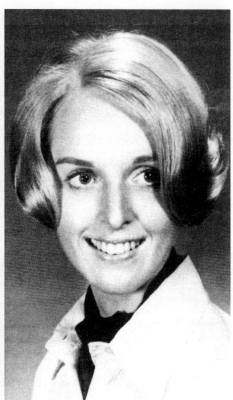

Bryan Hartnell (left) and Cecelia Shepard (right).

On the road, Bryan and Cecelia thought the late hour made the trip to San Francisco unwise, so they agreed to drive on to Lake Berryessa, a large man-made reservoir formed by the Monticello Dam built in 1957. The lake was 23 miles long, three miles wide, and surrounded by green hills. Bryan and Cecelia arrived at the isolated recreation spot, parked the Karmann Ghia on Knoxville Road, and walked down to the shoreline in an area known as Twin Oak Ridge.

They spread out a blanket on the grass by two large oak trees to enjoy the sunlight and scenery. After a time, Bryan heard a noise like the rustling of leaves and he asked Cecelia if she could see anything.

Lake Berryessa.

She noticed a figure walking among the clusters of trees on the hills above the shore.

"Oh, it's some man."

Bryan asked, "Is he alone?"

"Yeah," Cecelia replied. "Well, he just stepped behind the tree."

Bryan speculated that the man was looking for a place to relieve himself and then said, "Well, keep looking and tell me what happens."

Cecelia suddenly squeezed Bryan's arm. "Oh my God, he's got a gun."

The couple watched as the man emerged from the trees with a gun in one hand pointed directly at them. A dark, square hood covered his face and dark clip-on sunglasses were over the eye slits. He wore dark pants, a dark jacket, and heavy boots, with what may have been a wooden knife sheath on the right side of his belt near the front of his pants. The knife was long, with two brass rivets in the handle and cotton surgical tape wrapped approximately one inch around the grip. He also had a black holster fixed to his belt. A large, white crossed-circle was sewn onto the hooded costume over the man's chest. He walked across the grass and trapped the victims on the end of the peninsula.

The following account is taken from a transcript of the encounter written by Bryan Hartnell.

Cecelia shouted at the man. "What do you want?"

Police sketch of the killer in the hooded costume.

The hooded figure continued toward them. "Now, take it easy. All I want's your money. There is nothing to worry about. All I want is your money."

Bryan tried to remain calm. "Okay. Whatever you say. I want you to know that I will cooperate, so you don't have to worry. Whatever you say, we'll do. Do you want us to come up with our hands up or down?"

"Just don't make any fast moves. Come up slowly."

Cecelia and Bryan followed the man's instructions with their eyes locked on the gun in his hand.

Bryan tried to reason. "But we don't have any money. All I have is seventy-five cents."

"That doesn't matter," the stranger replied. "Every bit helps. I'm on my way to Mexico. I escaped from Deer Lodge prison in Montana. Deer Lodge. I need to get some money to get there."

"You're welcome to the money I have, but isn't there something else I can do for you? Give you a check or get some more?"

"No."

"I can give you my phone number and you can call me."

The man did not respond as Bryan rambled.

"I want to get in contact with you. I am a sociology major and maybe I can even offer you more help than you think you need."

The man refused. "No."

"Well, is there any other thing you need?"

"Yes," the man said. "One more thing. I want your car keys. My car is hot."

Bryan searched his pockets. "I guess in all the excitement I don't remember where I put them. Let's see. Are they in my shirt, in the ignition, on the blanket." He briefly considered trying to wrestle the gun away from the man. Bryan worried Cecelia might get hurt, but he still wanted to know if the gun was actually loaded.

"Say! Would you answer a question for me? I've always wondered. On TV movies and in an article in the *Reader's Digest* they say that thieves really keep their guns loaded."

The man seemed excited to answer, "Yes, it is!" He then added calmly in a matter-of-fact tone, "I killed a couple of men before."

Bryan was surprised. "What? I didn't hear you."

"I killed a couple of guards getting out of prison, and I'm not afraid to kill again."

Cecelia was terrified by the threat. "Bryan, do what he says!"

The stranger reached into his back pocket and pulled out some pieces of pre-cut plastic clothesline. "Now, I want the girl to tie you up."

Bryan tried to add some levity to the situation as he put his hands behind his back. "This is really strange. I wonder why someone hasn't thought of this before. I'll bet there's good money in it."

The man was silent as Cecelia tied the clothesline around Bryan's wrists. She reached into Bryan's pants pocket and tossed his wallet toward the man.

"What was the name of that prison?" Bryan asked.

The man did not respond, so Bryan pressed on. "No really, what did you say the name of it was? I'm just curious."

"Deer Lodge in Montana," the man answered begrudgingly.

Bryan thought there was more to the conversation, but he was unable to remember anything until he and Cecelia were both bound and the man said, "Now I want you both to lay face down, so I can tie up your feet."

"Come on," Bryan objected, "We could be out here for a long time and it could get cold at night."

"Come on! Get down!"

Bryan persisted. "Listen, I didn't complain when you tied our hands, but this is ridiculous!"

"I told you—"

"We aren't going anywhere. Anyway, I don't think that it's necessary."

The stranger pointed the gun directly at Bryan at point-blank range. "I told you to get down!"

Bryan noticed the man's hand slightly trembled. "Your hands are shaking? Are you nervous?"

"Yes, I guess so," the man laughed in a very relaxed manner.

"Well, I guess that I'd be nervous, too."

Cecelia and Bryan lay down on their stomachs and the man hog-tied them with more clothesline. The man's hands trembled as he tied Cecelia.

Bryan looked over his shoulder and asked, "Now that everything is all said and done, was that gun really loaded?"

"Yes, it was!" the man replied with delight. "I'll show you."

The stranger held the gun and ejected the clip to show Bryan the bullets inside. Bryan later said the ammunition resembled .45 caliber bullets. The man then put the gun back in his holster.

Bryan described what happened next. "And so I saw him put away his gun, and I was turning to say something to Celia, and all of a sudden I felt my back, just—no, I don't think I saw him pull it out. I don't remember. I think I saw him whip out his knife and just start stabbing me in the back... From the minute that knife blade went in, it was nothing but pure shock from there on. I mean I just did not expect it. I didn't expect that he would do that. That was a variable I had completely left out."

Cecelia watched in terror as the man plunged the long blade into Bryan's back again and again until Bryan pretended to be dead. The man then turned and attacked Cecelia, but she fought for her life and tried to avoid the blade when she turned over on her back. A Napa police report stated the "suspect went into some kind of frenzy" as he stabbed Cecelia approximately 10 times in her back, abdomen, and chest. The sudden attack abruptly ended. The man stood up, walked back to Knoxville Road, and stopped by Bryan's Karmann Ghia. He took out a black pen and drew a large crossed-circle on the passenger door along with the dates of the previous attacks as well as the date, time, and method of his latest crime.

Vallejo
12 - 20 - 68
7 - 4 - 69
Sept 27 - 69 - 6:30
by knife

The man climbed into his own car and drove away from the scene. Bryan and Cecelia realized that the stranger was gone and freed themselves from the pieces of plastic clothesline used to bind their hands. The couple prayed together.

Ronald Fong and his 9-year-old son sat in a small boat and cast their fishing lines as they drifted on the water near Goat Island. Bryan and Cecelia spotted the boat and shouted to get the fisherman's attention. Ronald heard faint voices, but he assumed someone was simply having fun somewhere. The voices got louder as the boat approached Twin Oak Ridge. Ronald noticed two figures on

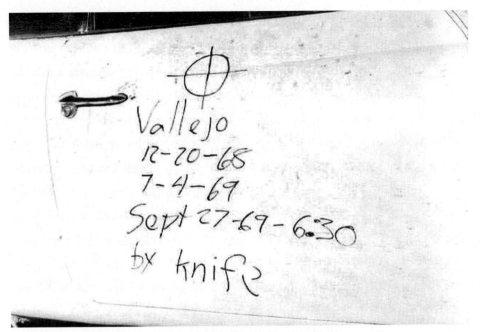

The message written on the door of Bryan Hartnell's car.

the shoreline and grabbed a pair of binoculars to get a closer look. He saw a man and a woman who were both covered in blood.

Bryan explained what happened and asked the fisherman to help them. Ronald was afraid his son was in danger and he did not want to remain in the area in case the attacker returned. He later recalled his dilemma when faced with the desperate victim. "He wanted me to go help him," Ronald said, "but I had my 9-year-old son with me." Ronald told the victims that he would go to the marina to get help. He then turned the boat around and headed north.

Bryan and Cecelia struggled to remain conscious as they lost more blood with each passing minute. Bryan decided they could not wait and set off on his own. "I was going to try my damnedest to stay alive," Bryan recalled. "Before I left her, I kissed her, and I said,

'Well, I'm gonna try to get help.'" He crawled almost 300 yards and collapsed near the road. A truck pulled up and park ranger Dennis Land stepped out to help the blood-soaked man. Bryan told Land to go help Cecelia, but the park ranger put him in the truck and drove to Twin Oak Ridge.

Ronald Fong stopped his boat at the marina and ran into the Rancho Monticello resort. He quickly found park ranger William White and told him about the horrific scene at the lake. Archie White (no relation) owned a boat repair shop and volunteered to take White and Fong to the location in his speed boat. Archie's wife, Elizabeth, joined the men and they soon arrived to find Cecelia on her hands and knees as she rocked back in forth in an effort to cope with the agonizing pain from her multiple stab wounds. Elizabeth tried to console the victim, but Cecelia begged to be knocked out or drugged to escape the pain.

Land helped Bryan out of the truck and they walked down to join the others. Ranger White went to Land's truck, picked up the radio microphone, reported the incident, and called for an ambulance. He then returned to the scene and asked the victims to explain what had happened. Bryan and Cecelia did their best to describe the man and the attack as they shivered in the cold air. The ambulance had a long trip from Napa to the crime scene and the victims could only hope they would survive until its arrival.

Dial M for Murder

Officer David Slaight was assigned to the switchboard at the Napa Police Department, approximately 27 miles south of Lake Berryessa. At 7:40 p.m., he answered an incoming call. "Napa Police Department, Officer Slaight."

He heard what sounded like the voice of a young man who spoke in a calm and deliberate manner. "I want to report a murder. No, a double murder. They are two miles north of park headquarters. They were in a white Volkswagen Karmann Ghia."

Slaight cautiously asked, "Where are you now?"

The voice quietly replied, "I'm the one who did it."

Slaight listened as the caller placed the receiver down, but the line remained open and he heard what sounded like female voices in the background. He called the Napa County Sheriff's Office and then called the phone company to ensure the operator kept the line open until the call could be traced. Pat Stanley, the news director of local TV station KVON, was at the sheriff's office when he heard about the call. He jumped into his car and drove around the area in search of the payphone in question. Stanley stopped to examine a phone booth at the Napa Car Wash at 1231 Main Street and noticed the receiver was off the hook. Police and the telephone employees quickly concluded that the call came from that booth with a telephone number that began with a 255 prefix. The booth was located a few blocks from the sheriff's office.

The ambulance finally arrived at Lake Berryessa and attendants Earl Trainor and Robert Parish rushed to the victims. Bryan and Cecelia were already in shock and weakened by the loss of blood, but the trip to the Queen of the Valley hospital in Napa would last an hour. Bryan was incoherent during the ride and Cecelia fell into a coma.

Ken Narlow was 39 years old, married with children, and an investigator for the Napa County Sheriff's Department. He finished dinner and was hoping to relax at home with his wife, but a telephone call with news about the stabbing at Lake Berryessa sent him back to work. At 8:33 p.m., Narlow joined his partner, Richard Lonergan, at the hospital and they met with Cecelia's mother, Wilma. They greeted the ambulance at 8:50 p.m., more than two hours after the attack. Cecelia was given a blood transfusion to stabilize her condition, so she was strong enough to undergo surgery. Hours later, both victims were taken to the intensive care unit. Doctors were confident that Bryan would fully recover, but they worried Cecelia might not survive.

Lonergan questioned Bryan about the suspect. Bryan described the man as heavy-set, possibly 200 to 250 lbs, but he was sedated and unable to provide more details. Bryan later said he could see brown hair through the eye holes in the hood. "I looked through his hair. It kind of looked like it was combed, you know, like this... it was brownish, you know, dark brown hair... He looked kinda heavy. I think he was weighing two and a quarter, two fifty, somewhere in there... I don't know how tall he was. Maybe 5-8 or maybe 5-10, 6 feet... His voice... I can remember... almost like I've heard it before. You know, there's some drawls that a lot of people have similar... And... almost as if I'd heard it before... couldn't think of where... It was just something, I guess his way of talking. It was something I couldn't repeat. It's like a song. Sometimes you know what you're going to say but you can't sing the melody worth a darn... But it was just a unique way of talking." Bryan also said the killer did not sound like an educated man. "He just impressed me as being rather low class. The reason was because of his clothes, you know."

Sergeant Hal Snook examined the phone booth at the Napa Car Wash. He dusted for fingerprints and discovered a fresh palm print on the receiver. Snook wrote in his report, "Heavy beads of moisture remained on the impressions" more than three hours after the caller had used the phone. Snook used a hot light to dry the print, so the impression could be lifted from the receiver. Ken Narlow later stated that investigators were "reasonably sure" that the palm print was left by the anonymous caller.

Narlow, Lonergan, and Snook traveled to Lake Berryessa and studied the crime scene at Twin Oak Ridge. Ranger Land reportedly collected everything at the scene in the blanket left by the victims. Bryan's Karmann Ghia was dusted for fingerprints, and the handwritten message was photographed and then covered with brown paper to preserve the evidence. A set of tire tracks approximately 20 feet behind Bryan's car may have been left by the killer's vehicle. The impressions were photographed and plaster casts were made of the tread design.

The next morning, investigators followed a trail of boot prints from the road, down to the crime scene, and back to Bryan's car. Plaster casts made of the prints and the boots were later identified as size 10½ "wing walkers" manufactured by the International Shoe Company in Philadelphia, Pennsylvania and shipped to the air force depot in Ogden, Utah, where they were then distributed to military installations only by written requisition order. The boots were sold in stores on the military bases. Five hundred to 1,000 pairs were sold as surplus, in addition to the boots sold on the bases. A hundred pairs of size 10½ boots were purchased and disposed of through sales between August 1968 and September 1969. The stores kept records of individuals who purchased the boots, but that information did not lead to any viable suspects.

A stranger is watching

Three students from Pacific Union College reported a strange encounter with a man at the lake on the day of the attack. Joanna,

21, and her two friends, both named Linda, went to Lake Berryessa to sunbathe around 3:00 p.m. Approximately two miles north of the A&W Root Beer stand on Knoxville Road, the girls parked their car and walked toward the shore. A car pulled into the area, quietly passed the girls, and then parked behind their car with the rear bumpers parallel. The vehicle was a late model, two-door, Chevrolet sedan, silver-blue in color with California license plates. The driver's head was down and the girls thought he was pretending to read something. They found a good spot, put their towels out, and laid down to enjoy the sunlight. Thirty minutes later, the girls noticed a

Detectives discuss the case with a composite sketch of a man seen at Lake Berryessa on the wall behind them.

man behind nearby trees. He seemed to be watching the bikini-clad girls from a distance of 40 to 50 feet. He walked toward them and was only 20 feet away until he turned and went up a hill.

Joanna and her friends described the man as 28 to 30 years old, with dark hair parted on the left side. He was at least six foot tall, with a stocky build, and weighed approximately 200 to 225 lbs. The man had a round face, rounded eyes, thin lips, a medium nose, straight eyebrows, and small ears. He was "nice looking," wore dark pants and a dark, short-sleeved sweater/shirt over an untucked white undershirt. The descriptions were used to create a portrait of the man with a selection of drawings of facial features, eyes, nose, hair, and other elements in the "Identi-Kit." The man was referred to as a "person of interest."

The description of the man was somewhat similar to the descriptions provided by Bryan Hartnell and Michael Mageau. Michael said the man at Blue Rock Springs Park was short, possibly 5ft 8in and real heavy set, possibly 195 to 200. Bryan said the man at the lake was heavy-set and 5ft 8in to 6ft tall, The three girls said the man was 28 to 30 years old, at least six foot tall, with a stocky build, 200 to 225 lbs.

Another possible report of the suspect came from Dr. Clifton Rayfield, a Los Gatos resident, who was with his 16-year-old son at the lake that day. Around 6:30 p.m., they walked along the shore approximately one mile away from the crime scene and saw a man 100 yards away. The stranger saw them and walked south up a hill. Dr. Rayfield said the man was about 5ft 10in tall, with a heavy build, wearing dark trousers and a dark long-sleeved shirt with some red color. Rayfield also saw a different man with two young boys, who carried guns, and the stranger may have been scared off by the presence of armed people in the area. The timing of Rayfield's sighting raised doubts about whether the stranger was the same man who attacked Bryan and Cecelia. Ken Narlow wrote in his report, "In the opinion of R/O's [reporting officers], it is unlikely, unless this male had a vehicle in the immediate area, he could have traversed the area to the scene of the crime on foot."

The sightings of the man at the lake led to the disturbing possibility that he was the same man who stabbed the victims and that he was looking for potential victims when he watched the three girls as they sunbathed. He may have decided not to attack the girls because trying to control three people would be too difficult. If he was the same man seen by Rayfield, he may have considered attacking the doctor and his teenage son. The behavior suggested anyone could be the next victim and the escalation of violence was even more terrifying if the stranger was the same man responsible for the "Zodiac" murders.

News reports linked the Zodiac to the stabbing at the lake and investigators believed one man was responsible for the crimes. Napa County Sheriff's Captain Donald Townsend called the Zodiac "a pathological, psycho killer," and said, "There is, as far as I'm concerned, a definite pattern between their killings and ours. The message left on the side of the victim's door, with the dates of the Solano County murders and ours, along with the other items that are on there, have definitely indicated to us that they're one and the same." Townsend added, "I'm sure that he realizes he needs help, medical help."

Growing bloodlust

The attack at the lake was a frightening departure from the Zodiac's previous MO. In his earlier crimes, the killer selected young couples sitting inside parked cars in secluded spots at night. The man at the lake targeted a young couple at an isolated location in daylight and he wore a bizarre, hooded costume. He talked with the victims, he left a handwritten message at the crime scene, and he used a knife instead of a gun. The savage knife attack indicated a marked increase in the killer's appetite for bloodshed.

Cecelia Shepard somehow survived the brutal stabbing, the long wait for the ambulance, the ride to the hospital, and hours of invasive surgery, but her brave fight ended when she died on September 29. Her body was taken to the Morrison Funeral Home and Dr. Dwight Straub and Dr. Wilmer De Petris conducted the autopsy. Cecelia had been stabbed ten times in the back, chest, and abdomen. Two of the wounds caused severe damage as the blade penetrated deep into the body. Straub and De Petris concluded the cause of death was severe brain damage due to severe cerebral anoxia, or a lack of oxygen to the brain, and severe internal hemorrhage caused by the stab wounds. Dr. De Petris believed that the murder weapon was a knife with a blade approximately nine to 11 inches long and one inch in width. The wounds indicated the blade was sharp on both sides like a military bayonet. Pieces of the skin including the wounds were preserved for comparisons with blades submitted as possible murder weapons.

Misinformation about Cecelia's wounds circulated immediately after the crime. A story published in the *Napa Register* on September 30 stated that Cecelia's wounds formed the pattern of a cross. *San Francisco Chronicle* reporter Paul Avery wrote that Cecelia was stabbed more than twenty times and the wounds formed the Zodiac's crossed-circle symbol. Bryan Hartnell and investigator Ken Narlow dismissed these stories, but factual errors regarding the Zodiac crimes were common and persistent.

During his interview with Detective John Robertson, Bryan described his wounds and said, "The doctor says there's six in the back, six wounds on my back." Bryan said the knife attack was sudden and without any warning, but park ranger William White's recall of Bryan's statements was very different. White spoke to the victims as they waited for the ambulance to arrive at the Berryessa crime scene. An official report included White's version of events: "Suspect stated he had to tie them up, and after they were tied the responsible said, 'I'm going to have to stab you.' White further related that the male victim advised the responsible, 'Stab me first. I can't stand to see (Cecelia) stabbed first.' The male victim advised that the responsible stabbed him numerous times in the back and then stabbed the girl." White later repeated the same story in an interview with a local television news crew. "The guy told him, he said, 'Take the money,' and he said, 'I don't want it.' He says. 'All I, all I want to do is kill you people. I have to kill ya.' The boy asked him, 'Do you really mean that?' and he said, 'Yes, I mean it.' Says, uh, he says, 'Well, if you're gonna, kill me first 'cause I can't stand to see the girl be stabbed.' Said, 'Well, I'll do that.' So he started stabbing the kid, in the back, he told me, ten, twelve times, but, uh, he had so much blood on him I couldn't tell. I know he was stabbed several times. And then he stabbed the girl."

According to Bryan Hartnell, the killer never revealed his intention to stab or kill the victims until he plunged the knife into Bryan's back. Bryan denied that he asked to be stabbed first. He later denied White's account and attributed the confusion to a misunderstanding and his incoherent state at the time. Bryan explained that he could only imagine saying something similar to White's account if he was describing his inner thoughts, such as, "I'm glad he stabbed me first because I wouldn't want to see Cecelia hurt."

The killer told Bryan and Cecelia he had escaped from a prison and killed a guard. Bryan told Detective Robertson the killer said the prison was in Montana, and Robertson suggested the word "lodge," an apparent reference to a prison in Deer Lodge, Montana. However, there was no record of any escape from Deer Lodge prison involving the murder of a guard. One man had escaped from the prison, but he was captured and did not match the description of the killer in the Zodiac crimes. In the summer of 1968, two convicts named Raymond Lee Wilson and David Finch escaped from the prison in Deer Lodge, Montana. They robbed a couple at knife point and stole a gun and their car. A story about the incident appeared in an issue of the military newspaper *Stars and Stripes* on July 24, 1968.

Ranger White told investigators that Bryan said the suspect claimed he escaped from a prison in Colorado. In his interview with Robertson, Bryan said, "[S]ome prison in Montana, I don't know the name of it is. Feathers? Do you know what the name of it is? I'll see if it sounds familiar. Fern or Feathers? It's some double name, like Fern Lock or something..."

Robertson quickly replied, "It's Lodge..."

"Oh, yeah, yeah, Lodge. At least we know we're together on that."

"Mountain Lodge Prison, or something of that nature," Robertson said.

Confusion created doubts about the "Deer Lodge" detail of the killer's story. Investigators wondered if Robertson had inadvertently planted the "Deer Lodge" element in Bryan's mind, although that was the location of the state prison in Montana.

The killer's fictional story about a prison escape made no sense if anyone checked the facts, but the lie was a logical ruse if he intended to scare the victims into cooperating until they could be bound and ambushed. The man at the lake said, "I killed a couple of men before... I killed a couple of guards getting out of prison, and I'm not afraid to kill again." He clearly believed telling the victims he was capable of killing would discourage them from any attempt to fight back or escape. He wanted to use the knife and that plan required him to control the victims until they were subdued and vulnerable. The story about the killing of a guard seemed designed to intimidate the victims, but the story about a simple robbery gave them a false sense of security until the moment the killer decided to strike. Talking with the victims allowed him to extend his anticipation of the surprise attack.

The killer may have changed his methods as he acted out his fantasies, adapted to his identity as a killer, and learned from his experiences. Details about the story of a prison escape and the strange costume would never have been known if both victims had died before help arrived, an indication that the costume was an important element of the killer's inner fantasy. The costume served his ego and was carefully created to enhance the "Zodiac" persona established by his earlier crimes and letters. The killer did not tell the victims that he was the Zodiac, perhaps because they would try to escape if he revealed his true identity or he enjoyed the secret knowledge of their impending doom. His behavior changed to accommodate his expanding fantasy life and his latest crime was so shocking that no one knew what he might do next.

Manhunt

Investigators Ken Narlow and Richard Lonergan attended the funeral services for Cecelia Shepard at the Pacific Union College Church in Angwin. They believed the killer might appear at the services, so everyone was photographed as they entered and exited the church. Narlow and Lonergan also accompanied the casket to the cemetery in St. Helena, but the surveillance did not identify any viable suspects.

The attack at Lake Berryessa forced the Napa Country Sheriff's Office and the Napa Police Department into the Zodiac story, along with the Benicia Police Department, the Solano County Sheriff's Office, the Vallejo Police Department and others. Cooperation among the many jurisdictions was essential and agents from the Bureau of Criminal Identification and Investigation (CI&I) were assigned to provide assistance. The California State Department of Justice provided necessary resources and guidance. Special Agent Mel Nicolai was assigned to coordinate the investigations and facilitate communications between the various law enforcement agencies. Supervising Special Agent Kenneth Horton worked with Nicolai to collect information and evidence in the three cases. Supervising Photographer Verne Menser documented the Zodiac letters, shell casings, bullets, bootprints, and more. Latent Fingerprint Examiner Raymond Olsen examined the palm print discovered at the Napa phone booth used by the killer, the palm print lifted from the door of Bryan Hartnell's car, and latent fingerprints found on the Zodiac communications.

Sherwood Morrill was a respected documents examiner and the head of the DOJ's Questioned Documents section. Some observers later criticized his conclusions in the case of Angela Davis, a member of the militant radicals known as the Symbionese Liberation Army (SLA). He was also involved in the cases of billionaire Howard Hughes and mass murderer Joan Corona. Morrill examined the Zodiac letters and concluded that one person was responsible for the writings, including the message left on the car door at Lake Berryessa. Decades of experience led Morrill to believe the killer used his natural hand printing and made no attempt to disguise or alter his handwriting.

On the morning of October 6, Nicolai, Horton, Menser, and Olsen met with Captain Donald Townsend at the Napa County Sheriff's Office. They discussed the evidence and the ongoing investigations of possible suspects. On October 9, investigators from the Napa County Sheriff's Office, the California Highway Patrol, the Solano County Sheriff's Office, and the DOJ met at the Vallejo police department to share information and possible leads.

On October 10, Mel Nicolai and Ken Narlow visited Bryan Hartnell at the PUC campus to check on his progress and confirm his account. Bryan had recovered physically, but he was haunted by the stabbing and Cecelia's death. He returned to classes and tried to resume his everyday life, but he still worried the Zodiac would kill again. In a television interview, Bryan said he underestimated the killer. "My first thought was that he was a sluggish, slow, rather stupid individual. I have been able to see by the way he operates that he is neither of these. Not that he is a genius, but he is definitely not stupid. He's got plans. I cannot believe that anyone normal could do the things he is doing."

OCTOBER 11, 1969—SAN FRANCISCO

Paul Lee Stine was born in Exeter, California on December 18, 1939. His parents, Theodore Milford Stine and Audra Thelma Stine, raised Paul with his older brother Joe and his younger sisters Geneva, Thelma, and Carol. In high school, Paul was known for his sense of humor and his reporting for the campus newspaper. He later worked for the Turlock journal before he enrolled in college. Paul took a job with the American United life insurance company to help pay the bills as he attended classes at San Francisco State college. He then fell in love with a young woman named Claudia Stark Wescott. She earned a bachelor of arts degree from the University of Wisconsin and worked as a statistician for the State of California Workmen's Compensation Insurance Fund. In May 1967, Paul and Claudia were married at the Cargill Methodist chapel in Janesville, Wisconsin. After their honeymoon, the couple returned to San Francisco and their home at 1842 Fell Street.

By the fall of 1969, Paul Stine was 29 years old and close to completing his graduate studies in English. He worked the 9:00 p.m. to 5:00 a.m. shift as a taxi driver for the Yellow Cab Company in San Francisco. After two months, he was eager to find other work and reportedly planned to change jobs.

Paul weighed 180 lbs, was 5ft 9in tall, with brown hair and brown eyes. On the night of October 11, 1969, he wore an undershirt, a white dress shirt with dark stripes, dark pants and matching jacket along with dark socks and shoes. He reported for a shift at the taxi garage at 8:45 p.m. and was assigned to cab #912, a yellow 1968 Ford Galaxie 500. He picked up his first fare of the night at Pier 64 on the east side of San Francisco and delivered the passenger to the airport. At 9:45, Paul answered a radio call from Leroy Sweet, the assistant traffic manager for Yellow Cab. He was directed to pick up a passenger at 500 9th Avenue in the Richmond district, located south of the expansive Presidio military base on the northern edge of the San Francisco peninsula. Sweet was concerned when Paul never arrived at the assigned address.

Paul Stine.

No one knew Paul's exact movements, but police speculated that he might have picked up a passenger somewhere around the intersection of Mason and Geary Streets. This location was near Union Square in the theater district, approximately 14 miles north of the airport and approximately 3 miles east of the pick-up location on 9th Avenue. Paul may have decided to take another fare along the way because the passenger's destination was close to the assigned address. Paul's trip book listed the destination as the intersection of Washington and Maple Streets, in the upscale residential neighborhood of Presidio Heights, approximately one mile northeast of 500 9th Avenue. For reasons unknown, Paul's cab was parked one block further west in front of the large house at 3898 Washington Street at the intersection of Washington and Cherry Streets.

On the second floor of the house across the street, three siblings were drawn to the window and saw a man in the front seat of the cab with the seemingly lifeless body of another man. According to a police report, 16-year-old Lindsey, his younger sister, Rebecca, and their younger brother, Trevor, contributed to a description of the man as a "white male adult, in his forties, 5ft 8in, heavy build, reddish blond 'crewcut' hair, wearing eyeglasses." They watched as the man on the passenger side of the cab appeared to search the victim's pockets. At some point, Lindsey went downstairs and peered through the window to get a better look at the man, while one of the other kids called the police. Inside the cab, the man pushed the body into an upright position behind the steering wheel. He then wiped around the interior and leaned over the body to reach the driver's compartment. The man climbed out of the passenger side, walked around to the driver's side, and continued to wipe at the exterior of the cab with "a white rag, possibly a handkerchief." He turned and walked north on

Cherry Street toward Jackson Street. Lindsey reportedly ran outside to the corner and observed the man's escape route.

Apparently, the first police radio broadcast about a possible robbery mistakenly described the suspect as a black male adult. SFPD never issued an official explanation for this error, but one theory blamed confusion during a frantic telephone call from a frightened teenager who may have described the suspect's clothing as black, but the police dispatcher somehow misheard that detail as the color of the suspect's skin.

Out of the darkness

Twenty-six-year-old San Francisco police officer Armond Pelissetti was on patrol with his partner, Frank Peda, when they heard the radio broadcast. They were the first officers who responded to the call. Pelissetti parked the police car directly behind the cab and noticed the three teenagers in the street. He quickly directed them back to their home and then turned to examine the cab. He approached with a flashlight in hand and noticed what appeared to be some smudges on the post between the front and rear doors on the driver's side. He directed the flashlight beam inside the cab and saw the lifeless body of Paul Stine. Pelissetti wrote in his report that the victim was "slumped over the front seat with the upper torso in the passenger side, head resting on the floorboard, facing north." The officer could see a large amount of blood in the interior of the vehicle and concluded the man was dead.

Pelissetti asked the three teenagers to describe the suspect and was surprised when they mentioned a white male adult. He radioed the correct description to headquarters and called for an ambulance and more officers to search for the suspect. Lindsey said the man walked north on Cherry Street, so Pelissetti told Officer Peda to guard the cab and headed up the sidewalk toward Jackson Street. He proceeded cautiously and shone the flashlight into the bushes along his path in case the suspect was hiding in the shadows.

Officer Donald A. Fouke, Badge #847, also heard the radio call that night. He had joined the police force in January 1964 and developed a reputation as a dedicated patrolman. On October 27, 1967, he responded to a robbery at a supermarket and chased an armed suspect on foot. The suspect fired shots at the officer and Fouke shot back until other people were in the line of fire. Fouke ran toward the suspect and kicked the gun from his hand. He was awarded the department's highest honor, the Gold Medal of Valor, and he was awarded a Bronze Medal of Honor in 1971.

On the night of October 11, 1969, Fouke was 30 years old and assigned to the Richmond Station. His regular partner was off duty, so Fouke was paired with a "rookie," 22-year-old, Eric Zelms, Badge #1348. The officers were in a patrol car northbound on Presidio Avenue, several blocks east of the crime scene, when they heard the radio broadcast. Fouke turned left and headed west on Jackson Street. He slowed the car as they came to the intersection of Jackson and Maple Streets, located one block northeast of Paul Stine's cab. Fouke estimated the speed of the patrol car was approximately 35 to 40 miles an hour when his eyes were drawn to his right as the headlights illuminated the figure of a man who was walking toward the patrol car on the north side of the street in the shadow of some trees. Fouke later described the suspect as a white male adult, approximately 35 to 45 years old, 5ft 10in tall, and approximately 180 to 200 lbs. The man had a crew cut and wore glasses, dark pants, and a dark jacket.

According to Fouke, he dismissed the white man who did not match the broadcast description of the suspect as a black male adult. The patrol car passed the man as he went up a flight of stairs toward the courtyard of a residence. Fouke estimated the entire sighting lasted no longer than 15 seconds.

Fouke said they passed the man and drove further west on Jackson Street to the end of the block when Officer Pelissetti appeared on the left at the southeast corner of Cherry and Jackson Streets. Pelissetti confirmed he saw Fouke and Zelms when he reached the corner. Fouke turned the patrol car south onto Cherry and stopped. Pelissetti told Fouke the initial description was wrong and the suspect was a white male. Fouke backed the patrol car onto Jackson and then drove west to the next intersection where he turned right onto Arguello Boulevard. He then turned right onto West Pacific Avenue and headed east in search of the suspect.

Fouke reported the sighting to headquarters along with his speculation that the man might have entered the Presidio grounds. Fouke believed the man may have acted as if he was entering the property of a residence simply to give the officers the impression he belonged in the neighborhood and then continued north on Maple Street after the patrol car drove away. Jackson Street served as a barrier between the Presidio Heights neighborhood and the Presidio military base. The houses along the north side of Jackson were bordered at the rear by a concrete wall at street level and a long drop down to the ground along the south side of West Pacific Avenue. Maple Street ran north and stopped at the wall. Anyone attempting to escape on foot would have had to jump from the high wall down onto the grass below. Fouke reasoned that the man continued north on Maple, jumped down, and ran across West

Pacific Avenue to the Julius Kahn playground or into the Presidio base.

The neighborhood flooded with more police officers, patrol cars, motorcycles, canine units, fire trucks, and spotlights. Sergeant Charles Beeme was in charge of the San Francisco Police canine unit and responded to the scene shortly after 10:30. He was disappointed to see so many people because the dogs would lose the scent of the suspect. Beeme and his dog partner, Darius, worked with five other dog handlers in a thorough but unsuccessful search of the Presidio grounds and the surrounding area. A description of the suspect would be broadcast continuously the next day.

San Francisco police inspector Walter Kracke joined Officer Peda in securing the crime scene. The taxi meter was still running at 10:46 p.m. and read $6.25. Police contacted the Yellow Cab Company and Leroy Sweet identified Paul Stine as the driver assigned to cab #912.

The crime scene at the intersection of Washington and Cherry Streets in San Francisco.

Ambulance #82 arrived and an ambulance steward called Dousette examined Stine's body on the passenger side of the cab. A large pool of blood had formed on the floor of the vehicle and Dousette could see a bullet hole on the right side of Stine's head between the temple and the ear. He pronounced the victim dead at 10:10 p.m.

Appointment with death

SFPD inspectors David Toschi and William Armstrong assumed control of the investigation at 11:10 p.m. Toschi was a San Francisco native and graduated from Galileo High School. He enlisted in the army to fight in the Korean War with the 24th Infantry Division. Toschi returned to the Bay Area and joined the San Francisco Police Department in 1953. He was promoted to the homicide division in 1966 and quickly developed a reputation as an ambitious inspector who enjoyed being in the spotlight. Toschi reportedly inspired actor Steve McQueen's portrayal of a tough SFPD Inspector in the 1968 film *Bullitt*. By October 1969, Toschi was 38 years old, married, and partnered with Bill Armstrong. The inspectors were already working on several homicides before they were assigned to investigate what appeared to be a relatively simple case of the robbery and murder of a cab driver.

Armstrong talked to the witnesses and obtained a description of the killer. Toschi inspected the cab and saw three red marks left on the seat by fingers covered in blood. He also discovered a small pair of black leather gloves in the back seat. A California Department of Justice report stated that the gloves were men's size seven, small for the hands of an average man.

Toschi searched Stine's pockets and found $4.12 along with other items but no wallet or cab keys. Robbery appeared to be a motive and

Toschi knew that taxi drivers were easy targets for robbers in search of a vulnerable source of quick cash. Eleven days earlier on the night of September 30, another driver for the Yellow Cab Company named Paul Hom picked up a passenger in front of the Fairmont Hotel. The passenger directed Hom to Washington and Locust Streets, then along Arguello Boulevard and into the grounds of the Presidio military base, where the man pulled out a gun and ordered Hom to stop the cab. He took Hom's cash and locked the helpless driver in the trunk of the cab with the false promise to call someone to set him free. Military police later heard Hom's cries for help and let him out of the trunk. Paul Hom described the robber as a white male adult, approximately 24 years old, 130 to 140 lbs, 5ft 9in tall with black hair, wearing a blue denim jacket and dark pants. The description did not match the description of the man who killed Paul Stine.

After the coroner's team removed Stine's body, Toschi discovered a copper-coated 9mm shell casing on the floorboard under the passenger seat. The inspector watched as the crime lab technicians processed the scene. Bill Kirkendal and Bob Dagitz located and collected fingerprints and impressions from the interior and exterior of the cab. They found latent prints, with traces of blood on the exterior post between the front and back doors on the driver's side of the cab. Officer Pelissetti said he saw these smudges on the post when he first approached the cab after the killer's escape. Investigators believed the fingerprints and others found on the handle of the passenger's front door most likely belonged to the killer. Dagitz and Kirkendal finished their work and cab #912 was towed away for further inspection.

San Francisco police officer Juan Morales later met with the teenage witnesses and developed a sketch of the killer based on their descriptions. The drawing was released to the public on October 13 with the description of the killer as a white male adult, 35 to 45 years old, 5ft 8in tall, with reddish-brown hair in a crewcut, wearing heavy-rimmed glasses and a navy blue or black jacket.

Claudia Stine was overwhelmed by the news that her husband had been murdered. She called Paul's brother Joe in Modesto and asked him to identify the body because she was too distraught. Joe and his friend, Michael Conway, drove to the San Francisco morgue and identified Stine for official records. Pathologist John C. Lee conducted an autopsy and examined the bullet wound on the right side of his head. The murder weapon was fired close to the victim's head and the heat and pressure burned the skin upon contact. An abrasion on the back of the victim's left hand may have been a possible defensive wound. Stine's blood-alcohol level was 0.02 percent, indicating he consumed at least one alcoholic beverage before his shift. The cause of death was listed as a "gunshot wound of the brain" as a result of homicide, and Paul Stine's body was cremated.

At the time, investigators believed robbery was the primary motive, and so one curious element of the killer's behavior was largely overlooked. Stine's clothing was collected as evidence, but part of his bloodstained dress shirt was missing. The back of the white shirt with vertical black stripes had been carefully cut into with a degree of precision and a large squared section was removed. This piece of cloth may have been the white rag or handkerchief held by the killer as reported by the witnesses. The shirt piece was apparently taken by the killer along with the keys to the cab, but an armed robber looking for money would have had little interest in these items. The killer's seemingly odd behavior indicated the theft of the missing shirt piece served another purpose beyond simple robbery.

WANTED

SAN FRANCISCO POLICE DEPARTMENT

NO. 90-69   WANTED FOR MURDER   OCTOBER 18, 1969

ORIGINAL DRAWING   AMENDED DRAWING

Supplementing our Bulletin 87-69 of October 13, 1969. Additional information has developed the above amended drawing of murder suspect known as "ZODIAC".

WMA, 35-45 Years, approximately 5'8", Heavy Build, Short Brown Hair, possibly with Red Tint, Wears Glasses. Armed with 9 MM Automatic.

Available for comparison: Slugs, Casings, Latents, Handwriting.

ANY INFORMATION:
Inspectors Armstrong & Toschi
Homicide Detail   THOMAS J. CAHILL
CASE NO. 696314   CHIEF OF POLICE

SFPD sketch of the killer as described by witnesses.

"I am the murderer"

"Please Rush to Editor" was written on the front and the back of an envelope delivered to the offices of *The San Francisco Chronicle*. Two six-cent stamps featuring President Franklin D. Roosevelt were on the upper right corner of the envelope postmarked October 13, and the sender placed a bloodstained piece of cloth inside, along with a letter written in blue ink.

> Dear Editor This is the Zodiac speaking I am the murderer of the taxi driver over by Washington St & Maple St last night, to prove this here is a blood stained piece of his shirt. I am the same man who did in the people in the north bay area. The S.F. Police could have caught me last night if they had searched the park properly instead of holding road races with their motorcicles seeing who could make the most noise. The car drivers should have just parked their cars & sat there quietly waiting for me to come out of cover. School children make nice targ-ets, I think I shall wipe out a school bus some morning. Just shoot out the frunt tire & then pick off the kiddies as they come bouncing out.

The letter was signed with another crossed-circle. Questioned Documents Examiner Sherwood Morrill examined the handwriting and concluded the letter was written by the same person responsible for the previous "Zodiac" messages. Criminologist John Williams confirmed the bloodstained piece of cloth was part of the section removed from the back of Paul Stine's shirt and analysis determined the blood matched the victim's blood type. The piece of shirt established a clear link between the person who murdered Paul Stine and the writer of the Zodiac letters.

> 1647710
>
> This is the Zodiac speaking. I am the murderer of the taxi driver over by Washington St & Maple St last night, to prove this here is a blood stained piece of his shirt. I am the same man who did in the people in the north bay a-ea. The S.F. Police could have caught me last night if they had

The Zodiac letter taking credit for Stine's murder.

The Chronicle published a piece about the Zodiac's letter with the headline, "Letter Claims Writer Killed Cabbie, 4 Others," but the newspaper withheld the threat to kill children. Schools were notified and bus drivers were given instructions on how to respond when under attack. Many law enforcement agencies deployed armed guards on buses, while patrol cars followed and aerial units monitored bus routes for any suspicious activity.

On or around October 15, the Santa Rosa Police Department received a telephone call from someone who reportedly claimed to be the Zodiac and made a threat about a bomb on a school bus. The massive effort to protect buses required explanation, so police finally revealed the Zodiac's threat to the public. On October 17, a driver for

Paul Stine's bloodstained shirt.

the Yulupa Elementary School in Santa Rosa heard what sounded like a gunshot from the left side of the bus. Police did not find any bullet holes or other impact damage on the exterior of the bus and none of the children onboard were injured. Some people believed the apparent knowledge of the withheld bus threat indicated the Zodiac was responsible for the call to Santa Rosa police and the shooting incident.

Investigators may have convinced the newspaper editors to withhold the information about the threat, but the Zodiac manipulated the police and the media as he forced them to react to his threat and thereby acknowledge his power. Hundreds of men were assigned to protect school children in response to one short paragraph written by the Zodiac. The headlines and television news reports terrified parents as children boarded school buses in fear of the invisible sniper.

The brutal crimes and taunting letters established the Zodiac's reputation as an anonymous killer, and no one had any reason to doubt he would act on his threat to murder children or that he was capable of doing so. San Francisco police captain Martin Lee warned reporters that the Zodiac was an extremely disturbed individual. "In his violent movements, or rather the violent periods that he has been in, he's an absolutely ruthless, completely merciless killer. He calmly goes about his business of, in one case telephoning the police and in another tearing a strip off the shirt of the dead body of the immediately killed victim. He doesn't get great excitement over it, he just thinks killing is just killing... This man is a psychopath, very, very seriously mentally deranged. He appears to have no conscience at all, no remorse after any of the acts, no reason or even alleged justification for anything that he does... He's a very, very sick and dangerous person."

The man who called himself the Zodiac unleashed a media circus and created a nightmare scenario for law enforcement. The killer crossed county lines into different cities and jurisdictions to involve several police and sheriff's departments as well as the California

Department of Justice and the FBI, and the investigation continued to expand as more agencies were drawn into the case. Each new crime and letter generated more media coverage and another wave of tips. Time and resources were wasted to check every lead, no matter how dubious or unbelievable. Authorities could not afford to let the killer escape justice because someone dismissed or ignored important information.

The sensational horror story attracted attention-seekers desperate to stand in the spotlight with opportunists, crackpots, imposters, and others who exploited the tragedy. Authorities were plagued by distractions and dead ends, and they faced heavy scrutiny as the hunt for the Zodiac became a public spectacle.

CHAPTER 2:
THE INVESTIGATION

"Then when they take on a persona through the media, they're motivated by a desire for—if I can— an anonymous fame."

FBI profiler Bill Hagmaier

Citizens of the Bay Area watched as the Zodiac created his persona of a bold and elusive killer with random murders, taunting phone calls to police, and threatening letters sent to newspapers. He seized control of the narrative and used his media access to mock police who allowed him to escape. The Zodiac's attempts to humiliate law enforcement became a central component of his communications, and he quickly became the most wanted man in the state of California after he expressed his desire to kill children.

In San Francisco, Captain Martin Lee directed inspectors Dave Toschi and Bill Armstrong to coordinate with the other jurisdictions involved in the investigation. On October 13, Vallejo police detective John Lynch sent a complete copy of the case file on the attack at Blue Rock Springs Park. Later that night, Toschi and Armstrong went to the Napa County Sheriff's Department to meet with Captain Donald Townsend, Sgt. Ken Narlow, and DOJ Special Agent Mel Nicolai.

They shared information and examined the evidence in all four cases. Ballistic comparisons determined the 9mm gun used to kill the cab driver was not the same weapon used in the Vallejo shooting. Napa investigators believed the palm print found on the payphone most likely belonged to the person who called police, and SFPD inspectors believed fingerprints found on the cab were probably left by the killer.

The Zodiac changed the investigation when he revealed his connection to the murder of Paul Stine. He made mistakes and risked arrest because he was seen by witnesses and police released a sketch of his face. He might be identified by fingerprints and the handwritten letter sent with a piece of the victim's bloodstained clothing established his guilt beyond doubt.

On Saturday, October 18, *The San Francisco Chronicle* printed a story written by staff writer Paul Avery headlined "Portrait of the Killer." Avery wrote, "The killer of five who calls himself 'Zodiac' is a clumsy criminal, a liar, and possibly a latent homosexual. That's the opinion of homicide detectives assigned to bring in the boastful mass murderer." The article insulted the killer yet also acknowledged his power. "But clumsy or a liar, Zodiac is still considered the most dangerous killer that Bay Area authorities can recall." Avery's assessment of the Zodiac may have been intentionally humiliating and deliberately designed to provoke a response.

Authorities seemed to concede their inability to catch the Zodiac with public pleas for him to surrender. Attorney General Thomas C. Lynch promised the killer would receive psychological treatment if he turned himself in to police. "We will see that the Zodiac gets help and that all his rights are protected. He is obviously an intelligent individual. He knows that eventually he will be taken into custody. So it would be best that he give himself up before tragedy is written in blood." *The San Francisco Examiner* also published a "Message to the Zodiac Killer" which included the statement, "We ask that you give yourself up, to *The Examiner*... And we offer to tell your story." The Zodiac did not respond to the message and he never wrote to *The Examiner* newspaper again.

Thomas Kinkead, Chief of the Riverside Police Department, saw news reports and suspected the Zodiac crimes might be connected to an unsolved murder in his jurisdiction. He contacted DOJ Agent Mel Nicolai and then called Sheriff Earl Randoll at the Napa County Sheriff's Department to discuss the details of the cases. Kinkead sent a package to Randoll with a letter describing the Riverside crime and photographs of messages attributed to the killer.

Death in a dirt driveway

The victim was 18-year-old Cheri Jo Bates. Born on February 4, 1948, in Omaha, Nebraska, she grew up in Southern California with her mother Irene, father Joseph, and brother Michael. An attractive girl with blond hair and blue eyes, Cheri Jo was a cheerleader and also made the honor roll at Ramona High School. Her parents separated in 1965, so Cheri Jo and her father moved into a small house at 4195 Via San Jose in Riverside, while Michael joined the Navy and was stationed in Florida. Cheri Jo graduated from high school and planned to become an airline stewardess. She attended classes at Riverside City College and worked at the Riverside National Bank.

In his letter to Sheriff Randoll, Chief Kinkead wrote, "On October 30, 1966, Cheri Jo Bates, a college student at Riverside City College, was brutally murdered. Our investigation revealed that the victim had gone to the city college campus to obtain some books from the library (the library was open on Sunday for the students' benefit).

It was established that she had entered the library and checked out three books at approximately 6:00 p.m. She returned to her vehicle in a dirt driveway between two houses. These houses were vacant and a part of the school property, having recently been purchased by the city college. While in this driveway area, our victim was attacked with a knife and stabbed numerous times in the chest. She was also stabbed once in the back, and her throat was severely cut, almost to the extent where she was decapitated. In addition to the stab wounds, our victim had been beaten about the face and had been choked. There was no evidence that the victim had been sexually attacked, as she was fully clothed and the clothing was not disarranged. There was nothing to indicate a motive of robbery, as victim's purse and its contents were intact. From all indications, the knife used by the suspect was one of approximately a ½ inch width blade by 3½ inches long."

Cheri Jo's Volkswagen Bug was parked in the library lot and the coil wire of the car's distributor had been pulled from its socket, an indication someone had tampered with the wires in an apparent attempt to disable the engine. Fingerprints were found on the car and greasy palm prints were discovered inside. In a report, Agent Nicolai provided information about a boot print found at the crime scene. "The heel print was identified as a B.F. Goodrich waffle design, men's four-eights inch washer type half heel. The B.F. Goodrich Products Division of Akron, Ohio, reported that this type of heel is sold only to the Federal prison industries at Leavenworth, Kansas. It was subsequently learned that Federal prison industries made low quarter military type shoes and supplied them to all of the armed services using black dress shoes. The measurement of the heel indicated that it would have been attached to an eight to ten size shoe. Shoes bearing the same type of heel were issued and sold at the PX at March Air Force Base at Riverside." Ten feet away from the body, police found a man's Timex wristwatch still running, but its black leather band was broken. Police speculated the killer might have left the watch behind after a struggle with the victim. Hairs were found in Cheri Jo's hand along with tissue under her fingernails.

Chief Kinkead saw similarities between the stabbing in Riverside and the Zodiac's knife attack at Lake Berryessa, but he believed the most compelling evidence of a possible connection was the so-called "Confession" sent to local police and the *Riverside Press-Enterprise* newspaper. The envelope was addressed by hand with a black pen, but the letter was typed.

She was young and beautiful. But now she is battered and dead. She is not the first and she will not be the last. I lay awake nights thinking about my next victim. Maybe she will be the beautiful blond that babysits near the little store and walks down the dark alley each evening about seven, or maybe she will be the shapely blue eyed brownett that said no when I asked her for a date in high school. But maybe it will not be either. But I shall cut off her female parts and deposit them for the whole city to see. So don't make it easy for me. Keep your sisters, daughters, and wives off the streets and alleys. Miss Bates was stupid. She went to the slaughter like a lamb. She did not put up a struggle. But I did. It was a ball. I first pulled the middle wire from the distributor. Then I waited for her in the library and followed her out after about two minuts. The battery must have been about dead by then I offered to help. She was then very willing to talk with me. I told her that my car was down the street and that I would give a life home. When we were away from the library walking, I said it was about time. She asked me "About time for what". I said it was about time for to die. I grabbed her around the neck with my hand over her mouth and my other hand with a small knife at her throat. She went very willingly. Her breast felt very warm and firm under my hands, but only one thing was on my mind. Making her pay for the brush offs that she had given me during the years prior. She died hard. She squirmed and shook as I choaked her, and her lips twiched. She let out a scream once and I kicked her head to shut her up. I plunged the knife into her and it broke. I then finished the job by cutting her throat. I am not sick. I am insane. But that will not stop the game. This letter should be published for all to read it. It just might save that girl in the alley... Yes I did make that call to you also. It was just a warning. Beware... I am stalking your girls now.

Information regarding the attempt to disable the victim's car was published in local newspaper articles. Police believed the writer's description of the murder itself was accurate. Chief Kinkead's letter to Sheriff Randoll stated, "The person who wrote the confession is aware of facts about the homicide that only the killer would know. There is no doubt that the person who wrote the confession letter is our homicide suspect."

"The Confession" was postmarked on November 30, 1966, one month after the Riverside murder. Approximately six months later, in April 1967, someone mailed three handwritten letters to Riverside police, the *Press-Enterprise* newspaper, and Cheri Jo's father, Joseph Bates. The letters read, "Bates had to die. There will be more," although the version sent to Mr. Bates read, "She had to die." The letters sent to police and the newspaper included a small symbol at the bottom of the pages which resembled the letter Z.

Documents examiner Sherwood Morrill later scrutinized the Riverside writings and concluded the "Confession" envelope and the three letters were written by the Zodiac, along with a morbid poem found on a desk in the Riverside City College library. Titled "Sick of living / unwilling to die," the poem seemed to recount or predict the "blood spurting" murder of a woman and ended with a taunting phrase, "Just wait till next time" and the initials "rh." Morrill's conclusion, linking the Zodiac to the poem, proved controversial as some critics questioned his findings.

Riverside police first proposed and embraced the Zodiac/Bates theory but later focused on a man who reportedly dated the victim and was upset when she ended the relationship. The police could not develop enough evidence to file charges against the man and the Zodiac remained an alternative suspect. Authorities did not reveal the "Riverside connection" to the public. The theory raised disturbing questions about the scope of the killer's crimes and the possibility his hunting grounds extended hundreds of miles away from the San Francisco Bay Area into Southern California.

Portrait of evil

On Monday, October 20, 1969, investigators gathered at the San Francisco Police Department to share information and further coordinate their efforts. Captain Martin Lee met with 27 people from nine different agencies, including Chief Assistant Attorney General Arlo Smith and DOJ Special Agent Mel Nicolai, Det. Sgt. Pierre Bidou of the Benicia Police Department, Steve Armenta of the State Bureau of Narcotics, SFPD fingerprint expert William Hamlett,

Det. Sgt. Hal Snook of the Napa County Sheriff's Office, and others from the United States Post Office, the California Highway Patrol, the Solano County Sheriff's Office, and the State Bureau of Criminal Identification and Investigation.

Captain Lee told reporters, "Our knowledge of each other's crimes wasn't as sharp as it might be, so we all met with the idea of sharing information, sharing evidence, and working together in the future, and part of the presentation was that representatives of each jurisdiction described in fine detail the particular crime that happened with him. I think we have a better picture of the suspect from this." A reporter asked if all of the crimes were committed by one person, and Lee replied that the evidence indicated "one suspect" was responsible for the attacks.

Dr. Lawrence Z. Freedman, Chairman of the Institute of Social and Behavioral Pathology at the University of Chicago, believed the Zodiac was "overwhelmed with terror" and desperately wanted to experience the intimacy enjoyed by his victims. Freedman also thought the killer was insane and suicidal, and that he wanted to be caught. Handwriting expert William F. Baker believed the Zodiac's writing indicated an unhappy childhood and hostility toward his mother. Baker was certain the killer was a paranoid schizophrenic who feared and hated the women he killed "to get back at his mother." He said the Zodiac threatened to attack a school bus because he was "a coward and feels that children can't hurt him." These psychological profiles seemed to confirm the popular assumption that the Zodiac was a deranged individual driven to kill by compulsions he could not control.

A dispatcher at the Oakland Police Department answered a call at 2:00 a.m. on Wednesday, October 22. The caller claimed to be the

Zodiac and requested that attorney F. Lee Bailey join host Jim Dunbar on the morning talk show broadcast from the KGO television studio in San Francisco. At the time, Bailey was best known for representing Albert DeSalvo, aka "The Boston Strangler," and accused wife-killer Sam Sheppard in a case that inspired the TV series *The Fugitive*. Bailey was based across the country in Boston, Massachusetts, and therefore unlikely to travel that distance in time to appear on the show, so the caller said he would accept notorious Bay Area lawyer Melvin Belli as a substitute. Belli was a high-powered celebrity who guest-starred on the science fiction TV series *Star Trek* and defended Jack Ruby, the man who killed the suspected assassin of President John F. Kennedy, Lee Harvey Oswald. The desk officer at Oakland PD called the KGO studio and explained the situation. He suspected the caller was an imposter and said, "He sounds really crazy, probably too crazy to be the Zodiac."

Melvin Belli was transported to the television station where armed police officers guarded the location in case the Zodiac was planning another attack. At 6:30 a.m., host Jim Dunbar explained that the Zodiac might call the studio and asked viewers to leave the telephone lines open for the killer. The phone rang at 7:10 a.m. during a commercial break, but the caller quickly hung up. He called back ten minutes later and spoke softly as he threatened to kill again if Belli did not help him. The caller hung up and then called back. He agreed to be referred to as "Sam" and wanted Belli to meet him on the roof of the Fairmount Hotel. Sam repeatedly hung up the phone to thwart police attempts to trace the call. In a series of short calls, Sam said he was sick, often had painful headaches, and was afraid of being executed in a gas chamber, the common method of capital punishment in the state of California at the time. One particular exchange indicated the caller might have developed an obsession with Belli.

> DUNBAR: Sam, let me ask you a question. Did you, um, did
> you attempt to call this program one other time when Mr.
> Belli was with us? And, you called...
> CALLER: What?
> DUNBAR: Did you try to call us one other time about, oh, two
> or three weeks ago when Mel Belli was with us?
> CALLER: Yes.
> DUNBAR: And you, uh, well...
> BELLI: You couldn't get through, and we were talking?
> DUNBAR: And you couldn't get through, the phones were tied
> up, is that it?
> CALLER: Yes.

Belli offered to speak to the district attorney on the caller's behalf, but Sam let out a loud scream and shouted, "I'm going to kill them. I'm going to kill all those kids!" Sam eventually agreed to meet Belli at the Church of Saints Peter and Paul on Mission Street at 10:30 a.m. Belli arrived at the location surrounded by police and reporters, but no one seemed surprised when Sam never appeared.

SFPD Inspectors Dave Toschi and Bill Armstrong doubted Sam was the Zodiac and they contacted the people who had spoken to the killer. Vallejo police dispatcher Nancy Slover, Napa police officer David Slaight, and surviving victim Bryan Hartnell listened to recordings of Sam's calls and unanimously agreed he was an imposter. Slaight thought Sam was too young to be the man who called the Napa Police Department after the stabbing at Lake Berryessa. Hartnell said the killer had a deeper voice and seemed older than Sam. According to Nancy Slover, Sam was not the same man who called the Vallejo police department after the shooting at Blue Rock Springs Park and he was "too pitiful and pathetic to be Zodiac." The Oakland police dispatcher also listened to the recordings and reportedly stated that Sam was the "really crazy" person who called that morning. Sam's television appearance was little more than a sensational distraction from the real investigation, but some people still believed he was the Zodiac.

The San Francisco Chronicle published a story headlined "A Target For Zodiac—Dare by Brother of Slain Man." Joe Stine, brother of victim Paul Stine, issued a challenge to the killer. He wanted to lure the killer into a trap and provided details about his daily routine, including his place of work and where he ate lunch. The grieving brother said, "Zodiac has to be sick, a maniac. I hope by offering myself as a target I can bring him out." Joe's public plea failed to provoke a response from the Zodiac who had been quiet since his last letter taking credit for Paul's murder.

The Zodiac's silence left everyone to wonder when and how he would return to the spotlight, and many people were afraid he would carry out his threat to attack a school bus. Vallejo Police Chief Jack Stiltz looked at the calendar and worried the killer might have a different plan to kill children. The upcoming Halloween holiday provided the perfect opportunity for the Zodiac to conceal his face with a mask and stalk more potential victims without creating suspicion. Stiltz urged parents to keep children inside because the killer might attack trick-or-treaters who came to his front door. Halloween was canceled for many disappointed kids because the community was terrified by the shadow of the Zodiac.

Murder by numbers

On November 8, a worker at a San Francisco post office unwittingly processed the next message from the Zodiac. Delivered to the offices of *The Chronicle*, the envelope had two six-cent Franklin D. Roosevelt stamps on the upper right corner. The Jesters greeting card inside featured an illustration of a dripping pen and the words, "Sorry I haven't written but I just washed my pen... and I can't do a thing with it." The card was produced by the Forget Me Not/American Greeting Cards Company, and the joke was a reference to a popular shampoo commercial with the catch-phrase, "I just washed my hair and I can't do a thing with it." The sender also added a handwritten message in blue ink.

> This is the Zodiac speaking I though you would nead a good laugh before you hear the bad news you won't get the news for a while yet PS could you print this new cipher on your front page? I get awfully lonely when I am ignored, So lonely I could do my Thing!!!!!!

A crossed-circle was accompanied by the notation, "Des July Aug Sept Oct = 7," which was interpreted by some as the number of victims, although there was no indication the Zodiac had killed anyone during the month of August. The cryptic entry led to assumptions the killer claimed responsibility for the murders of Kathie Snoozy and Debra Furlong in August, but the true meaning behind the Zodiac's vague hints was unknown. No one knew what the writer meant by "bad news," but the words "do my Thing" clearly implied more killing.

The Zodiac provided a new cipher constructed in 28 rows of 17 symbols to form a block of 340 characters. The code was similar to the Z408 cipher sent with the first letters in July, but the same key did not unlock the solution. Cryptography experts and amateur codebreakers could not reveal the hidden message and the cipher remained unsolved.

Another envelope was postmarked on November 9 in San Francisco and delivered to the *Chronicle* the next day. Two FDR six-cent stamps were placed in the upper right corner of the envelope, which contained another piece of Paul Stine's bloodstained shirt and a seven-page letter written in blue ink.

This is the Zodiac speaking Up to the end of Oct I have killed 7 people. I have grown rather angry with the police for their telling lies about me. So I shall change the way the collecting of slaves. I shall no longer announce to anyone. When I comitt my murders, they shall look like routine robberies, killings of anger, & a few fake accidents, etc. The police shall never catch me, because I have been too clever for them. I look like the description passed out only when I do my thing, the rest of the time I look entirle different. I shall not tell you what my descise consists of when I kill As of yet I have left no fingerprints behind me contrary to what the police say in my killings I wear transparent finger tip guards. All it is is 2 coats of airplane cement coated on my finger tips—quite unnoticible & very efective my killing tools have been boughten through the mail order outfits before the ban went into efect. Except one & it was bought out of the state. So as you can see the police don't have much to work on. If you wonder why I was wipeing the cab down I was leaving fake clews for the police to run all over town with, as one might say, I gave the cops som bussy work to do to keep them happy. I enjoy needling the blue pigs. Hey blue pig I was in the park—you were useing fire trucks to mask the sound of your cruzeing prowl cars. The dogs never came with in 2 blocks of me & they were to the west & there was only 2 groups of parking about 10 min apart then the motor cicles went by about 150 ft away going from south to north west.

This portion of the text was marked by brackets with the words "must print in paper."

ps. 2 cops pulled a goof abot 3 min after I left the cab. I was walking down the hill to the park when this cop car pulled up & one of them called me over & asked if I saw anyone acting suspicious or strange in the last 5 to 10 min & I said yes there was this man who was runnig by waveing a gun & the cops peeled rubber & went around the corner as I directed them & I disappeared into the park a block & a half away never to be seen again. Hey pig doesnt it rile you up to have your noze rubed in your booboos? If you cops think I'm going to take on a bus the way I stated I was, you deserve to have holes in your heads. Take one bag of ammonium nitrate fertilizer & 1 gal of stove oil & dump a few bags of gravel on top & then set the shit off & will positivily ventalate any thing that should be in the way of the blast. The death machine is all ready made. I would have sent you pictures but you would be nasty enough to trace them back to developer & then to me, so I shall describe my masterpiece to you. The nice part of it is all the parts can be bought on the open market with no questions asked.

1 bat. pow clock—will run for aprox 1 year

1 photoelectric switch

2 copper leaf springs

2 6V car bat

1 flash light bulb & reflector

1 mirror

2 18" cardboard tubes black with shoe polish in side & oute

the system checks out from one end to the other in my tests. What you do not know is whether the death machine is at the sight or whether it is being stored in my basement for future use. I think you do not have the manpower to stop this one by continually searching the road sides looking for this thing. & it wont do to re roat & re schedule the busses because the bomb can be adapted to new conditions. Have fun!! By the way it could be rather messy if you try to bluff me. PS. Be shure to print the part I marked out on page 3 or I shall do my thing To prove that I am the Zodiac, Ask the Vallejo cop about my electric gun sight which I used to start my collecting of slaves.

The writer had drawn a diagram of the proposed bomb and a crossed-circle with five Xs along the left side. Like the first letters mailed in July, the new message was written on bond paper with the Eaton brand watermark. The writer claimed to have killed seven victims, but only five murders were attributed to the killer at that time. Some people believed the crossed-circle with the five Xs represented the geographic locations of the Zodiac crimes on a map, while other theories suggested the markings indicated the locations of future attacks or some other potential clues.

Smoke and mirrors

The Zodiac's elaborate denials seemed like desperate attempts to cast doubt on the evidence, including the sketch of the killer and the fingerprints found at the crime scene. Eyewitness descriptions contributed to the sketch, but there was no indication the killer was wearing a disguise other than the dark-rimmed glasses, although he might have dyed his hair or used makeup to somehow distort his appearance. The Zodiac claimed he left "fake clews" as he wiped down the taxicab. Latent fingerprints with traces of blood were found on the exterior of the cab in the same area where the killer was last seen touching the vehicle near the driver's side door. Some theories suggested the killer used the severed hand of an unknown victim to leave fingerprints as a false clue to mislead police. Latent fingerprints are created by the oils and perspiration on the fingers of a living human being and are not visible to the naked eye like prints formed in blood. A pair of gloves discovered inside the cab may have been deliberately left behind to mislead police because a killer who claimed he applied airplane cement on his fingertips to create "transparent finger tip guards" had no need for gloves. The Zodiac claimed he was leaving fake clues as he was wiping down the cab, but that explanation made little sense because he could simply drop the gloves inside the cab.

After the murder of Paul Stine, the Zodiac mocked the police failure to catch him, but he never mentioned any encounter with officers. Instead, he mentioned the alleged incident almost as an afterthought buried in the text of the next letter sent almost a month later. The Zodiac complained that police were telling lies about him and he was obviously angry when they called him a clumsy liar. The Zodiac was determined to humiliate the police when he wrote, "Hey

pig doesnt it rile you up to have your noze rubed in your booboos?"
His story about the two officers seemed designed to portray them as
bungling incompetents fooled by a criminal genius. The Zodiac was
angry when police insulted him and he wanted to strike back, so he
may have remembered the passing patrol car and decided to invent
a self-serving story that would embarrass the police. No one could
prove the Zodiac lied about the encounter and police denials could be
dismissed as desperate attempts to avoid humiliation.

The Zodiac claimed that the officers asked if he had seen anything
suspicious or strange, but police were looking for a black male adult,
so they had no reason to seek out anyone else and instead would
just ask about anyone matching that description. In the Zodiac's
version of events, the officers sped away in the patrol car in search
of a man waving a gun, but Officer Donald Fouke said he stopped
the patrol car one block further west. Fouke's version was confirmed
by Armond Pelissetti, the first officer at the scene that night. Fouke
and his partner Eric Zelms never mentioned talking to any witness
or sighting an armed suspect on the loose in the immediate vicinity,
and they had no reason to withhold that information from Pelissetti
when their lives were in danger. Fouke and Zelms had no reason
to lie, but the Zodiac's story required that they decided to lie while
driving the distance of one block.

Years later, a book identified Fouke and Zelms as the officers who
stopped the killer but allowed him to escape. Fouke then appeared
in a television documentary and insisted he did not stop or talk
to the killer. He repeated his denials in other interviews and was
confronted with accusations that he was lying to cover up his own
incompetence. A police broadcast reportedly described the suspect
as a black male adult and the man allegedly stopped by Fouke was

white, meaning Fouke had a pretty good explanation for his failure to detain the individual, even if he had stopped and talked to the suspect as described in the Zodiac's letter. Fouke did tell Pelissetti he had seen a man who matched the corrected description of the suspect and he radioed dispatch to report what he thought might be the man's escape route.

SFPD Inspector Dave Toschi allegedly told one writer Fouke had confessed to stopping the Zodiac, but Fouke adamantly denied that story. Fouke claimed he saw the man and kept driving, but the Zodiac claimed the officers stopped and talked to him. Toschi's partner, Bill Armstrong, told a television producer that no one was sure if Fouke and Zelms had seen the Zodiac, an indication he made a clear distinction between seeing and stopping the suspect. Armond Pelissetti also claimed Fouke had confessed to him weeks after the murder, but Pelissetti later conceded he could not remember whether Fouke said he had stopped the Zodiac or that he was simply accused of doing so. Pelissetti did not believe Fouke stopped the killer because he would have noticed blood on the man's clothes. Fouke denied Pelissetti's claims along with an unconfirmed report that the widow of Officer Zelms later said he confessed to stopping the Zodiac and letting him go. According to the source of that story, Mrs. Zelms also complained that books contained "lies" about her husband, but those accounts stated that he and Fouke stopped the killer. Fouke's public and persistent denials made no sense if police reports and other witnesses could prove he was lying, but his statements were logical in a scenario where a best-selling book repeated the killer's version of events as fact and stories then adapted to the revisionist history. Whether or not he actually stopped the killer, Fouke was forever trapped in the Zodiac's version of the story.

On November 12, 1969, Officer Fouke wrote a memo regarding the sighting of the suspect.

Sir: I respectfully wish to report the following, that while responding to the area of Cherry and Washington Streets a suspect fitting the description of the Zodiac killer was observed by officer Fouke, walking in an easterly direction on Jackson street and then turn north on Maple street. This subject was not stopped as the description received from communications was that of a Negro male. When the right description was broadcast reporting officer informed communications that a possible suspect had been seen going north on Maple Street into the Presidio, the area of Julius Kahn playground and a search was started which had negative results. The suspect was observed by officer Fouke was a WMA 35-45 Yrs about five-foot, ten inches, 180-200 pounds. Medium heavy build– Barrel chested - Medium complexion– Light-colored hair possibly greying in rear (May have been lighting that caused this effect.) Crew cut– wearing glasses– Dressed in dark blue waist length zipper type jacket (Navy or royal blue) Elastic cuffs and waist band zipped part way up. Brown wool pants pleated type baggy in rear (Rust brown) May have been wearing low cut shoes. Subject at no time appeared to be in a hurry walking with a shuffling lope, Slightly bent forward. The subjects general appearance– Welsh ancestry. My partner that night was officer E. Zelms #1348 of Richmond station. I do not know if he observed this subject or not. Respectfully submitted. Donald A Fouke, Patrolman, Star 847.

Fouke's memo was the only official document about the Zodiac sighting available to the public. Unfortunately, Eric Zelms was killed on January 1, 1970, when two thieves took his gun and shot him. Decades later, Dave Toschi said Eric Zelms did not think the sighting of the man was "anything important," a strange comment if he had actually stopped the killer, allowed him to escape, and concealed the incident. Toschi never said Zelms admitted he and Fouke had stopped the Zodiac, and there was no public record of any report or statement by Zelms. SFPD lieutenant Tom Bruton was assigned to the Zodiac case years later and he read the department files. Bruton did not find any documents concerning the alleged Zodiac stop, and he believed Don Fouke told the truth.

Web of the Zodiac

The Zodiac's seven-page letter was designed to create more chaos and confusion, and his bomb threats further complicated ongoing efforts to protect school buses. Authorities did not have the resources necessary to search the entire Bay Area for explosive devices placed along bus routes. Investigators were disturbed by his references to children as the targets in his violent fantasies. They hoped he was bluffing and just wanted to scare people, but they also knew escalating threats could signal the killer was losing control.

The letter, card, and cipher were sent more than two weeks after Melvin Belli's televised conversation with "Sam," but the Zodiac was curiously silent regarding the imposter. Sam's exchange with Belli made national headlines, and a clip from the show was aired during the nationwide broadcast of the CBS evening news with anchor Walter Cronkite. Belli enjoyed the publicity and repeated his promises to help Sam. In late November, Belli was in Oklahoma City for a legal conference and he appeared on a local talk show broadcast from the KOCO television station. On December 7, a man who said he "could be" the Zodiac called the KTOK TV station in Oklahoma City. The news director said the caller did an "awfully good" impersonation of Sam.

The Oklahoma caller claimed he left California because he was too hot there. Shortly before someone claiming to be the Zodiac called the Oakland police on October 22, 1969, a man who claimed to be the Zodiac called the *Palo Alto Times* newspaper and said he left San Francisco to escape the heat. On December 7, 1969, someone in Fairfield, California mailed a letter to the *San Francisco Chronicle* newspaper, which read, "This is the Zodiac speaking I just need help I will kill again so expect it any time now the will be a cop than I will turn my self in OK." The writer also included a 38-symbol code which repeated elements of the previous Z340 cipher. Another letter, postmarked in Fairfield on December 16, 1969 and addressed to the *San Francisco Examiner* newspaper, featured a drawing of a large knife and drops of blood with the words, "The Bleeding knife of Zodiac." The letter read, "This is the Zodiac speaking I just want to tell you this state is in trouble I will go for the Government life so don't foreget me I will kill more people than you cops can count so look for more blood you better print." Several symbols and crossed-circles were followed by the words, "You will not catch me." The writer warned that more victims, including "cops," would be killed in San Francisco, San Jose, Vallejo, Napa, Fairfield, Sacramento, and Oakland. Unlike the Zodiac letters, the message was written on lined paper. On December 19, 1969, someone called the San Jose Highway Patrol and announced, "I am going to kill five of you officers and a family of five between now and Monday." The threat to murder police officers echoed the language of the Fairfield writer, and the Zodiac had already declared his hatred of law enforcement in published letters. Some aspects of the handwriting in the Fairfield communications were similar to the familiar Zodiac printing, but notable differences were also apparent. Unlike the Zodiac, the writer of the Fairfield letters used no punctuation, indented a first line of text, and did not include a dot with the lowercase letter "i" in most instances. Investigators were skeptical and suspected impostors were responsible for the telephone calls and the Fairfield letters.

Melvin Belli returned to the Bay Area to negotiate a deal for the legendary rock band The Rolling Stones to secure the Altamont Speedway as the location for a free concert with Jefferson Airplane and the Grateful Dead. On December 6, approximately 300,000 people descended on the speedway, more than 50 miles east of San Francisco, and the event quickly turned into a nightmare. The Hells Angels biker gang was hired as security and paid with a large supply of alcohol, but they were involved in several violent incidents. One of the bikers punched musician Marty Balin, and some audience members had gone wild by the time the Stones reluctantly took the stage. During a performance of the song "Under My Thumb," a man named Meredith Hunter pulled out a gun and moved toward the band. Biker Alan Passaro stabbed Hunter several items and faced criminal charges after the gunman died at the hospital. A camera crew filmed the concert for the documentary *Gimme Shelter*, and the footage proved Hunter pointed a gun at lead singer Mick Jagger before the stabbing. Belli assisted the Hells Angels and Altamont owner Dick Carter in securing Hunter's gun to support Passaro's claim of self-defense. Passaro was acquitted in January 1971, one month after *Gimme Shelter* was released in US theaters.

One year had passed since teenagers David Faraday and Betty Lou Jensen were murdered along Lake Herman Road on December 20, 1968, and the Zodiac marked the anniversary with a message to Melvin Belli. Postmarked in San Francisco on December 20, 1969, the envelope was addressed to the attorney's home in the city. The sender placed six one-cent stamps of President Thomas Jefferson in the upper right side of the envelope and included another bloodstained piece of cab driver Paul Stine's shirt inside to prove he was not an imposter. Belli was headed to Germany to attend a conference of military lawyers in Munich. On December 23, the envelope was delivered to his home on Telegraph Hill and then forwarded to his office where an employee discovered the message after the Christmas holiday.

Dear Melvin This is the Zodiac speaking I wish you a happy Christmass. The one thing I ask of you is this, please help me. I cannot reach out for help because of this thing in me won't let me. I am finding it extreamly dificult to hold it in check I am afraid I will loose control again and take my nineth & posibly tenth victom. Please help me I am drownding. At the moment the children are safe from the bomb because it is so massive to dig in & the triger mech requires much work to get it adjusted just right. But if I hold back too long from no nine I will loose complet all controol of my self & set the bomb up. Please help me I can not remain in control for much longer.

San Francisco police confirmed the bloodstained cloth was part of Stine's shirt. Documents examiner Sherwood Morrill concluded the letter was written by the Zodiac although the handwriting was initially uncharacteristically neat and straight but then reverted to a more slanted text near the end. The writer claimed he was losing control and begged for help, but skeptics questioned his sincerity and believed the letter was the product of the Zodiac's sick sense of humor.

During a long-distance telephone call from Rome, Italy on December 28, Belli told *Chronicle* reporter Paul Avery that he was confident the Zodiac would agree to a secret meeting and then surrender. The Zodiac never wrote to Belli again and the story was soon overshadowed by the next episode of the Zodiac circus.

Tunnel vision

In Chicago, Illinois, 44-year-old Italian immigrant and self-declared psychic Joseph DeLouise claimed he received vibrations from the Zodiac and believed the killer wanted to surrender. DeLouise flew to the Bay Area to consult with his "West Coast representative," Christopher Harris. They met with Mrs. Suennen, the mother of victim Darlene Ferrin. She believed Darlene might have been killed by her ex-husband James Phillips. He reportedly drove a 1963 Chevrolet Corvair, similar to the suspect vehicle described by surviving victim Michael Mageau. Mrs. Suennen said Phillips had an interest in astrology and could have received some training in codes during his brief service in the army. She also cited unsubstantiated rumors from family and friends that James had been in a mental hospital. When interviewed by Vallejo police detective Jack Mulanax, Mrs. Suennen repeated her suspicions and said Phillips and a pregnant woman attended Darlene's funeral. Mulanax wrote in his report that Mrs. Suennen "offered nothing new in way of factual information." Sgt. John Lynch contacted Joseph DeLouise and asked if he would like to examine Darlene's address book, but the psychic said he would return to Chicago instead.

James Phillips lived in Santa Cruz with his 28-year-old common-law wife, Shirley, and their five-month-old son. Detective Mulanax discovered Phillips was wanted for writing bad checks in Fairfield and had recently been arrested for outstanding traffic warrants. On February 2, 1970, Phillips arrived at the Santa Cruz Municipal Courthouse for his hearing and he was surprised when Mulanax appeared with a warrant for his arrest on charges of larceny. Mulanax took Phillips to the Santa Cruz Sheriff's Office and asked him to account for his whereabouts on the night of July 4, 1969. Phillips said he and Shirley hitchhiked to a "hippie encampment" in Boulder Creek, approximately 68 miles south of Vallejo. Shirley was also interviewed and confirmed the alibi. They had no means of transport because Phillips returned the 1963 Chevrolet Corvair when he could not afford the payments.

Mulanax asked about Darlene and Phillips said he accepted the divorce and moved on. He denied stories placing him at the funeral and claimed he did not know Darlene was dead until Mulanax revealed that information to him. He explained that he did not know Darlene changed her last name and therefore did not recognize the name in news reports about her death. Phillips denied any involvement in the murder and offered his full cooperation. He submitted to finger-printing, provided samples of his handwriting, and allowed police to search his home. James was 5ft 6in tall, weighed 160 lbs, with long brown hair, and he did not match the description of the man who killed Darlene. His fingerprints did not match any of the suspected Zodiac fingerprints and handwriting analysis indicated he did not write the Zodiac letters. Police did not find any evidence in his home. Mulanax effectively excluded Phillips as a suspect, and wrote, "It is opinion of R/O that Phillips is in no way connected with murder of Darlene Ferrin."

Christopher Harris held a press conference in Los Angeles with Vallejo mayor Florence Douglas, then a candidate for governor in a race against actor-turned-politician and future U.S. president, Ronald Reagan. Harris criticized police and suggested they had somehow bungled the investigation by ignoring important information which could solve the case. "I observed while in Vallejo that the police disregarded the ridiculous," Harris said. "I am now a firm believer that in the ridiculous, especially in the case of Darlene Ferrin, lies a storehouse of clues. The police should have done a complete character sketch of Darlene Ferrin. There are too many questions into her death that have not been properly tied down."

Harris later wrote, "While I was in San Francisco, January 1970, Darlene Ferrin's mother... called me and told me that the night her daughter was killed she told her mother as she left the house with her date, 'You might read about me in the papers in the morning.' The police in Vallejo did not seem to find much importance in Mrs. Ferrin's last words to her mother." Darlene's mother never mentioned this version of events to police. Investigators interviewed Darlene's family, friends, co-workers, and many others, but no one reported that Darlene made any similar statements. Darlene was at her own home and not at her mother's house when she left on the night of the murder and she picked up her "date" at his house. Investigators did not believe the story was true and they questioned Mrs. Suennen's failure to report Darlene's alleged statements in the six months after the murder. The story of Darlene's prophetic comment became the foundation for persistent theories that she was silenced by the killer before she could reveal some horrible secret.

Chasing the devil

The next sideshow began with the return of the Zodiac imposter known as "Sam." An FBI report dated January 14, 1970, stated: "On instant date Insp. *[name redacted]*, Homicide Detail, San Francisco Police Department, confidentially advised that UNSUB [unknown subject], who identified himself as 'Zodiac,' telephonically contacted attorney Melvin Belli's residence in effort to contact Belli. UNSUB was advised Belli was in Europe and stated, 'I can't wait. Today's my birthday.'"

Police set up a tape recorder and traced incoming calls to Belli's home. The man called several times but never stayed on the line long enough for the source to be located. On February 5, TV host Jim Dunbar was on air at the KGO studio when the station received another telephone call from "Sam." Due to a technical problem, only Dunbar's side of the conversation could be heard, but his responses revealed Sam's state of mind. At one point, Dunbar realized the caller was talking about the tragic events during the Rolling Stones concert at the Altamont speedway. Dunbar listened and replied, "Sonny Barger of Hell's Angels? Meredith Hunter? You are going to do it yourself to bring justice on the Meredith Hunter murderer?... You want Belli to represent you?... You want life in prison, not death?"

On February 18, 1970, San Francisco police informed the FBI that subsequent calls to Belli's house were traced to a mental institution and the caller was identified as a patient. In his summary of the case, Paul Avery named the caller as Eric Weil, an amateur photographer often seen at public events in the Bay Area. In 1965, Weil appeared at a televised press conference held by Bob Dylan. His questions and odd behavior revealed a fascination with a shirt worn by the singer in a photograph for an album cover. Eric's father was named

Sam, and Eric was born on January 10, around the time the Zodiac imposter said, "Today's my birthday!" Police compared Eric's voice to the recordings of Sam and concluded he was the man who called the television station and Belli's home, but he was not the Zodiac. The search for Sam was over, but police had wasted months of manpower and resources on a dead end.

The investigation was further complicated when 22-year-old Kathleen Johns arrived at the Patterson Police Department, more than 80 miles southeast of San Francisco, with a story about an encounter with a strange man. Kathleen lived in San Bernardino with her boyfriend, Robert, and their 10-month-old daughter, and she was pregnant with a second child. On the night of March 22, 1970, Kathleen decided to visit her sick mother in Petaluma, so she placed her infant daughter in a 1957 Chevrolet station wagon and began the hours-long drive to the North Bay Area. After she passed

Jim Dunbar and Melvin Belli on *AM San Francisco* discussing the calls from the Zodiac imposter.

Modesto and headed west on Highway 132, Kathleen noticed the driver of another vehicle kept flashing his headlights to get her attention. She ignored the car until they turned right onto Interstate 5 and headed north. The other car passed, so she pulled over and checked her vehicle. She watched as the other car stopped, backed up, and parked along the roadside. The driver was around 30 years old, 5ft 9in tall, approximately 160 lbs, with dark brown hair in a crew cut, wearing dark-rimmed glasses, dark pants, and a dark jacket. He approached Kathleen and said the right rear tire of the station wagon was wobbling, but he could fix the problem. Instead, he actually loosened the lug nuts, so the tire fell off when she tried to drive away. The good Samaritan then offered Kathleen a ride to a nearby service station and she accepted.

Kathleen grabbed her baby and climbed into the man's car, a light-tan, two-door American model with older California license plates. She believed they were headed to the ARCO station, but became concerned when the man did not stop there and drove off the highway onto back roads. The man was quiet, but Kathleen asked where he worked and he replied that he worked for two months at a time and liked to drive around at night. She asked if he helped other people and he replied that, when he was finished, they did not need any help.

In his report, Stanislaus County deputy sheriff Jim Lovett wrote, "Complainant stated that suspect was quite friendly with her, did not make any advances toward her, or threats toward her, and when asked if he was going to stop he would merely elude the question and start talking about something else." Kathleen said she sensed "The suspect intended to do some physical injury to her," but she never asked the man to stop the car and let her out. Sometime later, the car slowed down and she seized the opportunity, jumped out, and escaped on foot with her daughter. A passing motorist drove her to the police department. Deputy Lovett found Kathleen's station wagon near Interstate 5, along Highway 132 east of Bird Road. The vehicle had been set on fire in an apparent attempt to destroy evidence. Lovett noticed three lug nuts were missing from the right rear tire.

According to Sgt. Charles McNatt, Kathleen suddenly became hysterical when she saw the San Francisco police drawing of the Zodiac suspect in the police station. She said the abductor looked like the man depicted in the sketch, but her story created more problems for investigators. Johns said the man never threatened her or forced her to stay in the car, meaning there was no evidence the man committed any crime. Kathleen Johns might have encountered the Zodiac, but police most likely had no cause to arrest the man even if he could be identified. Doubts about Kathleen's story added to skepticism about any possible Zodiac connection.

The next day, the *S.F. Examiner* published a story about the so-called "Johns incident" with the headline, "Rode with Zodiac." Two witnesses contacted police with their own stories about a man in a car who tried to get them to pull over, but they continued driving. In his seven-page letter, the Zodiac announced he would change his MO, so authorities had to consider the possibility he was responsible for the failed abduction even though his behavior was drastically different than the previous attacks.

A game of death

In April 1970, lighting designer Robert Salem was murdered in his home at 754 Stevenson Street in San Francisco. The 40-year-old victim was stabbed dozens of times and almost decapitated. One of Salem's ears was missing and the killer used his blood to write the words "Satan Saves" and "Zodiac" on a wall. News reports focused on the bloody messages as a possible connection, but police did not believe the Zodiac killed Salem. Months later, the real killers were identified after a hit-and-run accident in Big Sur, California. Stanley Dean Baker, 22, and Harry Allen Stroup, 20, had the severed fingers of victims in their pockets when they were arrested. The men said they were cannibals and confessed to the murders of Robert Salem and other victims. Baker initially claimed he was part of a violent satanic cult, but he later admitted the story was not true and blamed his drug addiction for his crimes.

Another Zodiac message arrived at the *Chronicle* offices. Postmarked in San Francisco on April 20, the envelope featured two six-cent Franklin D. Roosevelt stamps and contained a new cipher.

This is the Zodiac speaking By the way have you cracked the last cipher I sent you? My name is— [13 symbols] I am mildly cerous as to how much money you have on my head now. I hope you do not think that I was the one who wiped out that blue meannie with a bomb at the cop station. Even though I talked about killing school children with one. It just wouldn't doo to move in on someone elses teritory. But there is more glory in killing a cop than a cid because a cop can shoot back. I have killed ten people to date. It would have been a lot more except that my bus bomb was a dud. I was swamped out by the rain we had a while back. The new bomb is set up like this

The second page included a diagram for the new "bus bomb" and a final note, "PS I hope you have fun trying to figgure out who I killed [crossed-circle] - 10 SFPD - 0."

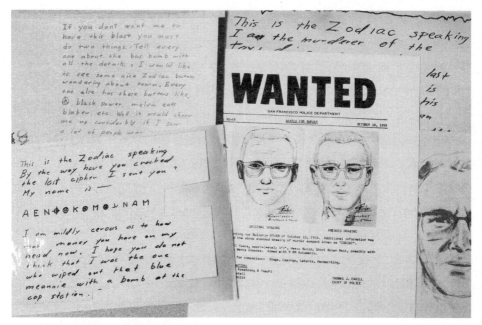

The Z13 "My name is" cipher.

The cipher may have been a response to a challenge issued by Professor D.C.B. Marsh of the American Cryptogram Association. In an article published in the *S.F. Examiner* on October 22, 1969, Marsh said the killer did not have the courage to reveal his identity and dared the Zodiac to send a cipher which "truly and honestly" included his real name.

The writer claimed ten victims, but did not mention the Johns incident or the murder of Robert Salem. "Blue meanie" was popular slang for police officers in Britain made famous in the animated Beatles cartoon *Yellow Submarine*, but protestors at the People's Park riots in Berkeley, California used the term to describe Alameda County sheriff's deputies in May 1969. The Zodiac referred to the bombing at a police station in Golden Gate Park two months earlier. Eight officers were wounded and Sgt. Brian V. McDonnell was killed in the explosion linked to extremists in the radical political group known as the Weatherman Underground Organization.

Authorities and newspaper editors withheld details regarding the bomb threats from the public, but the Zodiac was determined to get the attention he craved and sent another message to the *Chronicle* offices. Postmarked April 28, the envelope had two six-cent FDR stamps and contained a greeting card produced by the Jolly Roger company. The front of the card featured a cartoon of a prospector on a mule and another character on a tired green dragon with the caption, "Sorry to hear your ass is a dragon." In the upper right corner, the writer added, "I hope you enjoy your selves when I have my Blast. P.S. on back." The Zodiac's next threat was written on the back of the card. "If you don't want me to have this blast you must do two things. 1 Tell everyone about the bus bomb with all the details. 2 I would like to see some nice Zodiac butons wandering about town. Every one else has these buttons like, [peace sign], black power, melvin eats bluber, etc. Well it would cheer me up considerably if I saw a lot of people wearing my buton. Please no nasty ones like melvin's Thank you."

SFPD Inspector Bill Armstrong held a press conference and admitted the revelation of the Zodiac's threats was an attempt to appease the killer and deter him from using his bombs. "Now the reason we called this meeting was that it's obvious the suspect in this matter is referring to a bomb, and for some time we've had knowledge of this bomb from a letter we received on the 10th of November in which he indicated he is going to make a bomb, and in several letters which we've received since he mentions a bomb. For our own purposes, we had elected in cooperation with the press media not to publish this, but we feel at this time since there's an implied threat for the suspect this is something we might do." SFPD chief, Al Nelder, told reporters, "It is not my intention to frighten the public, but this guy has now demanded there be mention of the bomb and has threatened to blow up a school bus if mention wasn't made."

Code blue

In May 1970, San Francisco police submitted the collection of Zodiac messages to the FBI for analysis and bureau experts reported their conclusions. "Some of the threatening letters in this case, particularly [the December 20, 1969 letter and envelope to Melvin Belli] contain some distortion and were not written as freely as other threatening letters in this matter. Hand printing characteristics were observed, however, which indicate that all of the threatening letters in this case, including [the dragon card and envelope] were probably prepared by one writer." Another report included information about fingerprints found on the dragon card and envelope. "The enclosed photocopy of the card bearing Zodiac's message and envelope were furnished to San Francisco Office by Inspector [*redacted*], Homicide Detail, San Francisco Police Department. Inspector advised that the latent fingerprints were developed on the card and that to the best of his knowledge, the latents were not made by persons handling the card after its receipt by the *San Francisco Chronicle*. Inspector noted that the latents appearing on the envelope may have been made by personnel of the Post Office Department and *Chronicle* prior to its being turned over to the San Francisco Police Department."

On June 19, Vallejo resident Barbara Tagert contacted police to report a strange message delivered with her mail. The envelope was addressed to her husband, Gerald, and their home at 1423 Roleen Drive. Inside, the sender included a piece of paper with the words

"GIFT FROM ZODIAC," along with two tickets to the Oakland A's baseball game the next day. Vallejo police sergeant George Bawart noted the handwriting was somewhat similar to the Zodiac's, but there was no evidence to indicate the writer was the killer.

One week later, another envelope was postmarked June 26 with one six-cent FDR stamp and contained a handwritten letter as well as a map of the Bay Area. The writer had drawn a crossed-circle over the peak of Mt. Diablo in Contra Costa County with the numbers 0, 3, 6, and 9 at each of the four points and the instructions, "is to be set to Mag. N," an apparent reference to Magnetic North.

> This is the Zodiac speaking. I have become very upset with the people of San Fran Bay Area. They have not complied with my wishes for them to wear some nice ⊕ buttons. I promiced to punish them if they did not comply, by anilating a full School Buss. But now school is out for the summer, so I punished them in another way. I shot a man sitting in a parked car with a .38. The map coupled with this code will tell you where the bomb is set. You have untill next Fall to dig it up.

The Zodiac added a crossed-circle with the number "-12" on the upper right side, and the score, "SFPD - 0." Another crossed-circle was followed by a cipher consisting of 32 symbols at the bottom of the page.

Experts and amateurs studied the new code but were unable to decipher its hidden message. Authorities were skeptical of the writer's claim about a buried bomb, but they had to assume he was telling the truth and act accordingly. The Zodiac seemed emboldened by the public disclosure of his bomb threats and he may have been confident

This is the Zodiac speaking

I have become very upset with the people of San Fran Bay Area. They have **not** complied with my wishes for them to wear some nice ⊕ buttons. I promiced to punish them if they did not comply, by anilating a full School Buss. But now school is out for the summer, so I punished them in an another way. I shot a man sitting in a parked car with a .38.

⊕-12   SFPD-O

The Map coupled with this code will tell you whore the bomb is set. You have antill next Fall to dig it up. ⊕

C Δ J I ■ O X ⅃ A M ⅂ Δ Ω O R T G
X ⊙ F D V ℃ ⌷ H C E L ◈ P W Δ

The Z32 "Mt. Diablo code."

that police and newspapers would not censor his new letter for fear that he might retaliate by killing more victims.

Some observers believed the Zodiac's claim that he shot a man in a parked car with a .38 caliber gun was a reference to the murder of 27-year-old SFPD officer, Richard Radetich, in the early morning hours of July 19. Radetich parked his patrol car on the 600 block of Waller Street and was writing a citation for an Oldsmobile with expired plates when he was shot three times. A witness saw a man run away from the scene and tentatively identified Joe Wesley Allen Johnson, a career criminal and ex-convict who hated police. Johnson was arrested for murder but escaped prosecution due to a lack of evidence. Police were convinced Johnson killed Radetich and they did not believe the Zodiac was involved. *The Chronicle* published an article about the theorized connection with the provocative yet misleading headline, "ZODIAC SAYS HE KILLED SF OFFICER." Reporter Paul Avery wrote, "The Zodiac laid claim yesterday to the killing of Police Officer Richard Radetich." The Zodiac's vague reference to a victim shot in a car was interpreted as a direct confession but the evidence did not indicate he murdered Radetich or that he claimed the officer as a victim.

Confusion spreads

Sensational news stories inspired speculation about the Zodiac's possible connection to other crimes, and his next letter only created more confusion. The envelope mailed to the *Chronicle* was postmarked in San Francisco on July 24 with one six-cent FDR stamp.

This is the Zodiac speaking. I am rather unhappy because you people will not wear some nice ✠ buttons. So I now have a little list, starting with the woeman + her baby that I gave a rather intersting ride for a couple howers one evening a few months back that ended in my burning her car where I found them.

The letter was an obvious reference to the failed abduction of Kathleen Johns four months earlier, but the confession only contained details already known to the general public, including the location where Kathleen's burned station wagon was found. Some investigators suspected the Zodiac used that information and claimed credit for the abduction to pad his criminal resume.

Kathleen Johns was later interviewed by Paul Avery and others, but her accounts of the incident appeared to change over time. An article printed in the *Los Angeles Times* quoted Kathleen's new story that the man threatened her and said, "You know I'm going to kill you. You know you're going to die." According to a police report, Kathleen never mentioned the man's threats when she was interviewed immediately after the incident. She said the man "was quite friendly with her, did not make any advances toward her, or threats toward her." In her new story, the man also threatened to throw her baby out of the car window. Kathleen originally said she escaped and the man did not follow, but she later claimed he yelled and chased after her. The contradictions and apparent embellishments cast doubts on Kathleen's stories and raised questions about her credibility. The Zodiac's letter did not provide any answers.

Two days after he sent the letter claiming credit for the Johns abduction, the Zodiac mailed another message to the *Chronicle*. The envelope was postmarked with one six-cent FDR stamp in San Francisco on the night of July 26th. In five pages of handwriting in blue ink, the Zodiac quoted lyrics from the popular musical *The Mikado*.

This is the Zodiac speaking Being that you will not wear some nice ⊕ buttons, how about wearing some nasty ⊕ buttons. Or any type of ⊕ buttons that you can think up. If you do not wear any type of ⊕ buttons, I shall (on top of everything else) torture all 13 of my slaves that I have wateing for me in Paradice. Some I shall tie over ant hills and watch them scream & twich and sqwirm. Others shall have pine splinters driven under their nails & then burned. Others shall be placed in cages & fed salt beef untill they are gorged then I shall listen to their pleass for water and I shall laugh at them. Others will hang by their thumbs & burn in the sun then I will rub them down with deep heat to warm them up. Others I shall skin them alive & let them run around screaming. And all billiard players I shall have them play in a darkened dungen cell with crooked cues & Twisted Shoes. Yes I shall have great fun inflicting the most delicious of pain to my slaves SFPD=0 ⊕ =13 As some day it may hapen that a victom must be found. I've got a little list. I've got a little list, of society offenders who might well be underground who would never be missed who would never be missed. There is the pestulentual nucences who whrite for autographs, all people who have flabby hands and irritating laughs. All children who are up in dates and implore you with im platt. All people who are shakeing hands shake hands like that. And all third persons who with unspoiling take thoes who insist. They'd none of them be missed. They'd none of them be missed. There's the banjo seranader and the others of his race and the piano orginast I got him on the list. All people who eat pepermint and phomphit in your face, they would never be missed They would never be missed And the Idiout who phraises with inthusastic tone of

centuries but this and every country but his own. And the lady
from the provences who dress like a guy who doesn't cry and
the singurly abnormily the girl who never kissed. I don't think
she would be missed Im shure she wouldn't be missed. And that
nice impriest that is rather rife the judicial hummerest I've got
him on the list All funny fellows, commic men and clowns of
private life. They'd none of them be missed. They'd none of them
be missed. And uncompromiseing kind such as wachmacallit,
thingmebob, and like wise, well—nevermind, and tut tut tut tut,
and whatshisname, and you know who, but the task of filling up
the blanks I rather leave up to you. But it really doesn't matter
whom you place upon the list, for none of them be missed, none
of them be missed.

A large crossed-circle was drawn on the page with the words: "PS.
The Mt. Diablo Code concerns Radians & # inches along the radians."

Written in 1884 by dramatist W. S. Gilbert and composer Arthur
Sullivan, *The Mikado* was still a long-running favorite musical in
the Bay Area during the 1970s. The Zodiac quoted lyrics from the
song "I've Got a Little List," but his version was slightly different than
the original text. He may have heard that recording of the song as
presented in the soundtrack album for the 1960 television production
for *The Bell Telephone Hour*, starring comedian Groucho Marx. The
song is sung by the character Koko, the Lord High Executioner, as he
ponders who will be his next victim.

The Zodiac referred to radians, a term usually associated with
higher mathematics. A radian is an angle valued between 57 and
58 degrees, an angle subtended by an arc of a circle equal in length
to the radius of a circle. The radian is the standard unit of angular

measure, but the degree is more commonly used in surveying and navigation. A circle consists of 360 degrees, 6.28 or 2pi radians. Degrees can be converted into radians by multiplying the number of degrees by pi/180. The Zodiac may have hoped his hints about radians and inches would help experts unlock the hidden message and reveal the location of the buried bomb, but the "Mt. Diablo code" remained unsolved. Like the 13 symbol "My Name Is" cipher sent in April 1970, the code of 32 symbols was too short for cryptographers to use the same method of searching for similar repeated patterns that helped crack the first cipher in August 1969.

Technicians at the San Francisco police crime lab examined the pages of the Zodiac's newest letter and discovered latent fingerprints, as reported by an FBI memo dated July 31, 1970. "Several days ago, two additional letters were received by a local newspaper. Handwriting comparison indicates these last two letters are from the same individual. Eight latent fingerprints were developed from one of the letters. These prints are from two different pages... It is possible to determine the pattern of each of the prints. All are individually identifiable with the possible exception of the print that is believed to be the right little finger. Six of the latent prints were developed on the letter in a position that indicates they are impressions of the middle, ring and little fingers of the right and left hand. Two of the latent prints may be of the thumb or index finger of the right hand and left hand... Elimination prints have been obtained of all persons connected with the newspaper and the Police Department who could have possibly handled the letters. The latent prints have not been eliminated."

The FBI also stated an inspector at the SFPD lab reported that a fingerprint from a letter matched another fingerprint found at a crime scene. "On July 30, '70, the San Francisco Police Department Inspector of the crime lab advised that he believes the left ring-finger latents noted on the enclosures bears similarity to bloody fingerprint removed from door of vehicle driven by victim taxi driver." Matching fingerprints from a letter and a crime scene would establish a definitive link between the writer and the killer, although sending pieces of a victim's bloodstained clothing with the letters already proved the writer was connected to the murder. The lack of further documentation or confirmation regarding the fingerprint match cast doubts on the inspector's conclusion.

Endgame

A card sent to the *Chronicle* on October 5 appeared to be another communication from the Zodiac. The sender used a paper punch to create 13 holes on one side of the card. One Apollo 8 Moon Orbit stamp featuring the words "In the beginning God..." was placed on the front and the text was on the other side. The message was composed of letters and words clipped from newspaper articles and other sources.

> DEAR EDITOR: You'll hate me, but I've got to tell you. THE PACE ISN'T ANY SLOWER! IN FACT IT'S JUST ONE BIG thirteenth 13 Some of Them Fought It Was Horrible' Zodiac P.S. THERE ARE REPORTS city police pig cops are closeing in on me. Fk I'm crackproof, What is the price tag now?

On Friday September 25, 1970, the *Oakland Tribune* and other newspapers published the daily entry of the comic strip *Smidgens* by artist Bob Cordray. A character says, "The pace isn't any slower! In fact it's just one big sprawling subdivided rat race." Some words were cut from the strip and pasted onto the "Zodiac" postcard message.

The absence of the familiar handwriting raised doubts about the authenticity of the card, although the punched holes may have been a reference to the previous message mailed on July 26. In the "Little List" letter, the Zodiac wrote that he would torture all 13 of his slaves. The *Chronicle* did not publish that letter and the reference to 13 slaves was not known to the general public. Both the card and the previous letter were finally published on October 12.

Another card was sent to the *Chronicle* on October 27 and arrived the following day. Postmarked with one Apollo 8 Moon Orbit stamp, the envelope was addressed to "Paul Averly" and contained a Halloween card manufactured by the Gibson Greeting Cards company. The front of the card included the words, "FROM YOUR SECRET PAL– I feel it in my bones, You ache to know my name, And so I'll clue you in– ." On the inside, the message read, "But then why spoil the game! Happy Halloween!" The sender pasted a grinning skeleton with fingers that formed the "OK" sign and the number 14 was written on the palm. An orange pumpkin was placed over the skeleton's pelvis. The writer added the words, "Boo!" and "4-TEEN," as well as a crossed-circle, the letter "Z," and 13 wide eyes. Another symbol appeared inside the card and on the front of the envelope in place of a return address. The words "PARADICE" and "SLAVES" were written on the back of the card to form a cross, with "BY FIRE, BY GUN, BY ROPE" and "BY KNIFE" in each of the four sections. The letter "N" in the word knife was inverted to resemble the letter "Z."

Chronicle employees contacted police and Avery was informed that the message seemed to suggest he could be the 14th victim.

Some of the newspaper staff joked about the situation and wore buttons which read, "I AM NOT PAUL AVERY," but the danger was real. Avery bought a .38 caliber revolver for protection. The reporter soon found himself pointing the gun at a knife-wielding man who was harassing a citizen, and Avery realized he could not kill another human being. He stopped carrying the gun and learned to live with the possibility the Zodiac could strike at any time.

Death notice

A story about Avery and the Halloween message prompted a citizen to write a letter to report his theory that the Zodiac might have been responsible for the 1966 murder of Riverside college student, Cheri Jo Bates. Avery contacted Riverside Police Captain Irv Cross and then flew south to collect photographs of the writing linked to the Bates case. Documents examiner Sherwood Morrill concluded that the Zodiac was responsible for the messages as well as a morbid poem written on a desk found in the Riverside City College library. "The handwriting scratched on the desk is the same as on the three letters, particularly like that on the envelopes, and this hand printing is by the same person who has been preparing the Zodiac letters received by the *Chronicle*."

Thomas Kinkead, chief of the Riverside Police Department, first named the Zodiac as a possible suspect in October 1969, but many accounts later credited Avery as the first to discover the link between the two cases. *The Chronicle* published Avery's story about the "Riverside connection" in November and created another news frenzy. Headlines read, "Evidence Links Zodiac Killer to '66 Death of Riverside Coed," although some investigators were skeptical of the theory. Napa County sheriff's detective Ken Narlow, DOJ agent Mel

Nicolai, and SFPD inspectors Dave Toschi and Bill Armstrong met with Riverside police and shared information.

Police expected the killer would respond to the publicity surrounding the Riverside revelations, but the Zodiac disappeared after sending the Halloween card to Paul Avery. Months passed before he finally resurfaced with a letter mailed to *The Los Angeles Times* newspaper. The envelope was postmarked on March 13, 1971, in Pleasanton, California, approximately 40 miles southeast of San Francisco. Two six-cent FDR stamps were placed upside-down in the upper right corner and the sender wrote the words, "AIR MAIL," on the back.

This is the Zodiac speaking Like I have allways said, I am crack proof. If the Blue Meannies are evere going to catch me, they had best get off their fat asses & do something. Because the longer they fiddle & fart around, the more slaves I will collect for my after life. I do have to give them credit for stumbling across my riverside activity, but they are only finding the easy ones, there are a hell of a lot more down there. The reason I'm writing to the Times is this, They don't bury me on the back pages like some of the others. SFPD-0 [crossed-circle] -17+

The phrase "riverside activity" was immediately interpreted as a confession to the Bates murder, but some skeptics believed the Zodiac took advantage of the opportunity and claimed credit for a crime he did not commit. The vague reference to other unknown victims inspired endless speculation linking the Zodiac to many unsolved crimes.

Postal workers had been on the alert since the Zodiac's first letters in July 1969, and they searched for possible Zodiac communications in the daily routine of sorting through incoming mail. Days after the letter was sent to the *LA Times*, an agent noticed a peculiar postcard featuring cut-and-paste letters addressed to *"The Times," "S.F. Examiner,"* and *"The San Francisco Chronicle."* Like the Halloween message, the sender misspelled the reporter's last name and wrote, "Att. Paul Averly." A hole was punched into the upper left corner with the handwritten word, "Zodiac," and one four-cent President Abraham Lincoln stamp was placed in the right corner. An illustration of a snowy setting and a man with a shovel was glued to the other side of the card with the pasted phrases, "Peek through the pines," "Sierra Club," "around in the snow," and "pass Lake Tahoe areas." The illustration had been clipped from an advertisement for a condominium project known as "Forest Pines" at Incline Village in the Tahoe area. The sender also included the words, "Sought victim 12."

Investigators wondered if "victim 12" was a reference to a young nurse who disappeared from the Tahoe area in September 1970. Twenty-five-year-old Donna Lass was 5ft 4in tall, 135 lbs, with blue eyes and blond hair. She lived in an apartment in Stateline, Nevada and worked at the Sahara Hotel and Casino. Donna finished her shift on September 5 and then apparently vanished. According to some accounts, Donna's boss and her landlord received telephone calls on September 7 from a man who falsely claimed she had to leave town due to a family emergency. No one who knew Donna could believe that she would go away without contacting family or friends, and police suspected she was dead. Donna's car was found in the lot outside her apartment, an indication she might have been abducted after she arrived home. The unidentified caller was the prime suspect, but the case remained unsolved. Some people believed the postcard was a clue about the location of Donna Lass or another unknown victim, and the image of the man with a shovel suggested a body might be buried somewhere near Incline Village. Theories involving the Zodiac noted that, in May 1970, Donna lived only a few blocks away from the scene of the San Francisco murder.

The Zodiac's box score entries implied he claimed 17 victims, yet there was no evidence he had killed anyone since October 1969. He seemed to lose interest in communicating and apparently stopped sending letters, ciphers, and clues. In his early messages, the Zodiac was so desperate that he threatened to kill if newspapers did not give him the attention he wanted. By the summer of 1971, he walked out of the spotlight and silently returned to the shadows. The man who terrorized the Bay Area for two years was suddenly gone, but the nightmare continued for those trapped in the aftermath of the Zodiac.

CHAPTER 3:
THE AFTERMATH

"The evil that men do lives after them;
the good is oft interred with their bones."
William Shakespeare

The killer's absence created a vacuum as citizens, investigators, and the media adapted to life in the post-Zodiac world. Forgers, hoaxers, amateur sleuths, and those accused as suspects filled the void, and police struggled to cope with the remnants of the cold case. Without its main character to drive the narrative, the legend of the Zodiac was absorbed into popular culture.

Tom Hanson, owner of several Pizza Man and Kentucky Fried Chicken restaurants, spent $13,000 to produce and direct a low-budget film about the case, titled *The Zodiac Killer. Chronicle* reporter Paul Avery wrote a brief introduction and the fictional story focused on Jerry, a postman who kills innocent victims and taunts police. Jerry hangs out at a diner and is interested in a young waitress, a character apparently inspired by real-life Zodiac victim Darlene Ferrin.

Hanson's film ran for one week in April 1971 at the RKO Golden Gate Theater in San Francisco, and the director created a plan to catch the killer. Moviegoers could win a free motorcycle by explaining why the Zodiac killed. Written answers were dropped into a large box and a man inside quickly checked for Zodiac-like handwriting in case the real killer made an appearance. In the theater restroom, Hanson encountered a man matching the Zodiac's description, who casually informed the director that blood did not come out of a human body as depicted in the film. Hanson believed the man was the Zodiac and launched his own amateur investigation.

The Zodiac offered no public comment on Hanson's production or the other movie he inspired, the 1972 classic thriller, *Dirty Harry*, starring Clint Eastwood as Harry Callahan, a San Francisco police inspector called into action when a psychopathic, extortionist killer known as Scorpio hijacks a school bus filled with children. In December 1972, the Zodiac was reduced to a punchline in an episode of the television sitcom series *Sanford and Son*, titled "*The Light Housekeeper*." Fred Sanford begged his son not to leave him alone because "they never did catch that Zodiac killer."

Suspect zero

The Zodiac had eluded police for more than two years, but investigators were cautiously optimistic when an informant identified a new suspect. Arthur Leigh Allen was born on December 18, 1933, in Honolulu, Hawaii. He grew up in Vallejo with his older brother, Ron, his mother, Bernice, and his father, Ethan, a retired naval commander. Leigh graduated from high school in 1951 and later joined the Navy in 1956. He was stationed at Treasure Island in the San Francisco Bay, but was discharged after he was found drunk in his car with a gun. Leigh briefly worked at the Travis Air Force Base near Fairfield, California until he was found in his car with alcohol and a weapon. He later earned a degree and became a teacher, but his career ended due to what some euphemistically described as his "problem with children." In March 1968, Allen was fired from his teaching job at Valley Springs Elementary school after complaints of sexual misconduct with students. In April 1969, he lost another job at a Vallejo gas station after making "improper advances" toward the owner's young daughter.

By the fall of 1969, Allen worked as a janitor at the Elmer Cave Elementary School in Vallejo. On October 6, Vallejo police detective John Lynch interviewed Allen at the school and asked him to account for his whereabouts on September 27, the day of the Zodiac attack at Lake Berryessa. Allen stated that he had considered going to the lake on the 26th but instead went skin diving at Salt Point Ranch, located more than 80 miles northwest of Vallejo. Allen lived with his parents at 32 Fresno Street in Vallejo, but he could not remember if they were there when he returned from Salt Point on the afternoon of the 27th. He said he remained at home for the rest of the day. Allen was described as bald, 6ft 1in tall with a heavy build, weighing approximately 241 lbs. Lynch documented the interview in his report but did not mention the reason for the interest in Allen or how his name first surfaced in the investigation.

In July 1971, Don Cheney contacted police after he saw a newspaper article about speculation that the Zodiac was responsible for a brutal machete attack at the Dog Bar campground in the Sierra Mountains, 35 miles northeast of Sacramento. Years earlier, Cheney shared a house with Allen's brother, Ron, when they were attending Cal Poly State College in Pomona. Don developed a friendship with Leigh and they enjoyed fishing, diving, and hunting together, but the relationship reportedly ended after Allen allegedly touched one of

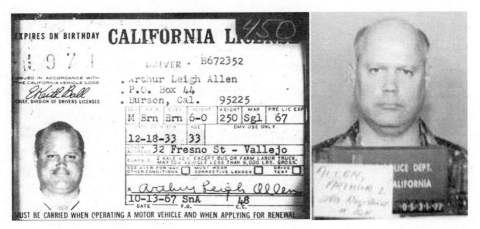

Arthur Leigh Allen.

Don's children in an inappropriate manner. Cheney did not tell police about this incident, but he later claimed he was concerned and kept his children away from Allen. Ron Allen said Don angrily confronted him about Leigh's behavior, but Cheney later dismissed the incident as insignificant and said he had never discussed the issue with Ron. Police wondered if Cheney's seemingly incredible story was an attempt at revenge against Allen.

Don Cheney told police that Allen made incriminating statements during their last visit sometime around New Year's Eve 1967. Cheney said Allen was upset about losing his teaching job and talked about hunting people using a gun with a flashlight attached to the barrel. Cheney claimed Allen said he would target couples in lovers lane areas and then write taunting letters signed with the name "Zodiac." He said Allen also talked about shooting at a school bus and picking off the "little darlings," language similar to the Zodiac's threat to shoot "kiddies." Cheney said he was disturbed by Allen's murderous fantasies and decided to end their association. If true, Cheney's story demonstrated Allen had prior knowledge of the Zodiac crimes.

The details in Cheney's story had been published in news reports about the case and he did not offer any new information. Some elements of the story raised questions about Cheney's timing of events. Allen lost his job in March 1968, after Cheney said he last spoke to Allen in December 1967, so Cheney changed the date of the conversation to December 1968. In later interviews, Cheney said he was aware of the Zodiac crimes in 1969 and, at the time, even noted that a sketch of a man seen at Lake Berryessa resembled Allen, but he did not recall the disturbing conversation that prompted him to end his friendship with Allen ten months earlier.

Vallejo police detective Jack Mulanax, SFPD inspectors Dave Toschi and Bill Armstrong, and DOJ Agent Mel Nicolai gathered information about Allen and interviewed people who knew him. Allen's father died in March 1971 and Leigh lived with his mother in the house on Fresno Street in Vallejo, although he sometimes stayed in trailers and various other locations. Allen was also ambidextrous and could write with both hands. The suspect reportedly talked about *The Most Dangerous Game*, a popular story about a man who hunts human beings for sport. Allen's friend and former co-worker, Philip Tucker, told police that he once saw Allen holding a paper with some symbols, although this sighting occurred months after the Zodiac's ciphers were published in newspapers. Police also investigated the possibility that Allen had used one of Tucker's cars during the shooting at Blue Rock Springs Park, but they concluded he most likely did not have access to the vehicle at the time.

Police learned Allen worked as a junior chemist at the Union Oil refinery in Pinole, and they arrived unannounced to interview him there on August 4, 1971. Mulanax, Toschi, and Armstrong were surprised to see the suspect wore a Zodiac brand wristwatch featuring a crossed-circle. Ron Allen told police their mother Bernice had given Zodiac watches to both brothers as Christmas gifts in December 1967. Allen said he initially followed the news stories about the Zodiac case, but eventually thought the coverage was morbid. When asked if he ever made statements about hunting human beings, Allen said he may have discussed the story *The Most Dangerous Game,* but he did not remember making the statements attributed to him by Don Cheney. The investigators were stunned when Allen referred to bloody knives on his car seat on the day of the stabbing at Lake Berryessa. He explained that he met a couple at Salt Point Ranch and used the knives to kill chickens they cooked for dinner. The unprompted admission seemed incriminating, but Allen denied any involvement in the crimes.

Ron Allen and his wife Karen were surprised that Allen was a suspect in the Zodiac case. They knew Leigh was a child molester but did not believe he was a killer. Ron told police that Don Cheney was a reliable person, but he also mentioned Don's anger about the alleged molestation incident in the context of Cheney's credibility. Ron and Karen believed Cheney invented the story about the "Zodiac" conversation to implicate Leigh as revenge for the incident. Karen said Leigh used the phrases "trigger mech" and "Merry X-Mass," similar to language in the Zodiac letters. The investigation failed to produce any evidence to justify a warrant to search the home Leigh shared with his mother, so Ron and Karen agreed to search his room and report back to police.

On Saturday, August 7, 1971, Ron and Karen visited the house on Fresno Street and quietly informed Leigh about their encounter with police. At first, Leigh seemed to enjoy the police attention, but he later came to view the spotlight as a curse. Ron and Karen believed

Leigh when he denied the accusations, but they still returned to the house on August 14 and searched his basement room. Ron told police there was some "cryptogram-type material," which he could not say was related to the Zodiac. Karen inspected the contents of a gray metal box, including some letters and papers with some symbols which she later said were not similar to the Zodiac ciphers. The search yielded no evidence and the investigation effectively stalled until September 1972, when San Francisco police obtained a warrant to search Allen's trailer at the Sunset Trailer Park in Santa Rosa. Allen had permission from the state to experiment on animals as part of his studies to earn a degree in biology, and he kept a small freezer containing the dead bodies of squirrels. Police also found a large dildo, two handguns, and an M-1 rifle. Allen no longer enjoyed the unwanted attention and he quietly cooperated as the men completed the search.

Allen denied making incriminating statements to Don Cheney, and he seemed surprised to learn his former friend was behind the accusations. The suspect was finger-printed and he provided samples of his writing with both hands. Documents examiner Sherwood Morrill examined a collection of Allen's handwriting samples and concluded the suspect did not write the Zodiac letters. A comparison proved Allen's fingerprints did not match the suspected Zodiac fingerprints. Allen did not match the physical description of the killer. Some investigators may have believed Allen was the Zodiac, but the evidence indicated otherwise. After a year of investigation, police moved on to pursue other suspects. In later interviews, Armstrong and Toschi stated that fingerprints and handwriting could identify the Zodiac even after that evidence did not match Allen.

Killing time

On August 1, 1973, a letter was sent to the *Albany Times-Union* newspaper in Albany, New York.

> YOU WERE WRONG I AM NOT DEAD OR IN THE HOSPITAL I AM ALIVE AND WELL AND I'M GOING TO START KILLING AGAIN Below is the NAME AND LOCATION OF MY NEXT VICTIM But you had Better hurry be-cause I'm going to kill her August 10th at 5:00 P.M. when the shift change. ALBANY is A Nice Town.

The writer signed the message with a crossed-circle and also included a cipher, which apparently contained the name and location of the next victim. Police did not believe the letter was written by the Zodiac and the handwriting was not similar. A man who claimed to be the Zodiac contacted law enforcement and news agencies on January 11, 1974. The caller said he killed a woman and directed police to find the body in a church somewhere in Daly City, located more than 20 miles south of San Francisco. Every church was searched, but no body was found and police dismissed the calls as a hoax.

Investigators were constantly distracted and disappointed by Zodiac impostors, so many were skeptical of reports the killer sent a new letter to *The Chronicle* newspaper. The envelope was postmarked on January 29, 1974, in San Francisco, with one eight-cent stamp of President Dwight D. Eisenhower turned on its left side and several stamp-book stickers placed at the bottom.

> I saw + think "The Exorcist" was the best saterical com-edy I have ever seen. Signed, yours truley: He plunged him self into the

billowy wave and an echo arose from the sucides grave titwillo titwillo titwillo

Unidentified symbols were drawn below the main text with the box score "Me = 37 SFPD = 0." The final lines were lyrics from the musical, *The Mikado*, interpreted by some as a suggestion the writer planned to commit suicide. The blockbuster horror movie *The Exorcist* was released on December 26, 1973, with screenings at the Northpoint Theater near Fisherman's Wharf in San Francisco. On January 11, 1974, *The Chronicle* ran Paul Avery's article on the audience reaction to the film about the demonic possession of a young girl. The writer most likely saw the movie at the Northpoint theater and the new letter may have been a response to Avery's article.

The writer did not use the name "Zodiac," but the handwriting was sufficiently similar to raise suspicions the killer might have returned. Police submitted the letter to the FBI for analysis and a bureau expert concluded the message was "probably prepared" by the author of the Zodiac letters. The killer's apparent return was major news, and SFPD inspectors Dave Toschi and Bill Armstrong answered calls from excited reporters and sorted through a wave of new tips. Investigators wondered if the box score was accurate and the Zodiac had actually killed 37 people, but they were unable to identify any previously unknown victims.

A message sent to the *Chronicle* on or around February 3, 1974 was postmarked with one eight-cent Dwight D. Eisenhower stamp.

Dear Mr. Editor, Did you know that the initials SLAY (Symbionese Liberation Army) spell "sla," an old Norse word meaning "kill." A friend

I saw + think "The Exorcist" was the best saterical comidy that I have ever seen.

Signed, yours truley :

He plunged him self into the billowy wave and an echo arose from the sucides grave tit willo tit willo tit willo

Ps. if I do not see this note in your paper, I will do something nasty, which you know I'm capable of doing

Me - 37
SFPD - 0

The "Exorcist" letter sent in January 1974.

The radical militant group known as the SLA had been in the headlines after they assassinated Marcus Foster, superintendent of Oakland Public Schools, in November 1973. Two SLA members were arrested for the murder on January 10, 1974, two weeks before the arrival of the *Exorcist* letter. Newspaper heiress Patty Hearst was kidnapped by the SLA on February 4, 1974. Someone connected to the SLA sent a letter to the Hearst family, which was also signed "A friend." Some people believed the use of the word "friend" indicated both letters were written by someone in the SLA and not the Zodiac. The person who mailed the SLA letter used a President Eisenhower stamp like the one sent with the *Exorcist* letter. Results of handwriting analysis were inconclusive, with FBI experts noting "some characteristics which are not entirely consistent" with the Zodiac's writing but also stating that "no characteristics were found which would definitely establish [the SLA letter and envelope were] prepared by someone other than the writer of the Zodiac letters."

Another message sent to the *Chronicle* was postmarked in Alameda County on May 8 with one eight-cent stamp of American "founding father," Samuel Adams. A handwritten letter complained about advertisements for a new film loosely based on the case of spree killer Charles Starkweather and his 14-year-old female companion Caryl Ann Fugate.

Sirs - I would like to express [crossed out "ion"] my [crossed out "consterate"] consternation concerning your poor taste and lack of sympathy for the public, as evidenced by your running of the ads for the movie "Badlands," featuring the blurb "In 1959 most people were killing time. Kit & Holly were killing people."

In light of recent events, this kind of murder-glorification can only be deplorable at best (not that glorification of violence was ever justifiable) why don't you show some concern for public sensibilities & cut the ad? A citizen

An envelope postmarked in San Rafael, CA, on July 8, with one ten-cent Famous Works of Art stamp featuring Spanish painter Francisco Goya, contained a letter complaining about *Chronicle* columnist "Count Marco" Spinelli. The initials "R.P." were written on the upper left side of the envelope instead of a return address. The handwritten letter featured long strokes and flourishes different than the Zodiac writing.

Editor – Put Marco back in the hell-hole from whence it came -- he has a serious psychological disorder -- always needs to feel superior. I suggest you refer him to a shrink. Meanwhile, cancel the Count Marco column. Since the Count can write anonymously, so can I -- The Red Phantom (red with rage)

The signature may have been a reference to the 1907 silent movie *El Spectre Rojo*, aka *The Red Phantom*, however the name also appeared in a letter sent to Count Marco in 1962. The writer apparently responded to the columnist's comments about women. "Dear Count Marco: Instead of sneaking up on women like a red phantom with black paint, you should work openly and usefully to help this free and generous country which feeds your nasty face. Chicago." Count Marco replied, "Red phantom?! I'll have you know I wear gold Chinese silk or gold Italian raw silk evening jackets, and I don't sneak. I go about town in them, openly so you will be sure to see

me. In fact, I'll be in Chicago on December 5 to give you a personal look at me, so be prepared."

The name Red Phantom could have been a possible clue as to whether the Zodiac sent the letter, but the odd handwriting led some to conclude the message was just another hoax. Like the other communications in 1974, the "Count Marco" letter was the subject of ongoing debate amid doubts about its authenticity. Impostors cast a cloud over the case and demonstrated that the Zodiac was losing control of the narrative. The world no longer needed him to keep the story alive and the legend took on a life of its own.

Work of the Devil

On the night of July 29, 1974, the St. Vincent Ferrer Roman Catholic Church in Manhattan's upper west side of New York City was engulfed in flames. A 71-year-old priest was killed in the fire which police believed was the work of an arsonist. Shortly after the fire broke out, a man who claimed to be the Zodiac killer called the United Press International office and the *New York Daily News*. The caller warned that he was "unleashing a tirade against the Catholic church. Priests are going to die. Someday people will realize that Christianity is a fraud." After more fires at other churches, police arrested 56-year-old Gordon Earl Marais, a transient veteran with a history of severe mental health problems. Detectives described Marais as "a very nice guy" who claimed he was a genius CIA agent and an informant for the FBI. He requested psychiatric treatment and was committed to Bellevue Hospital. Marais was wanted in California for theft from a department store and he faced multiple charges of burglary, arson, and homicide in New York. Police concluded that Marais was responsible for the telephone calls to UPI and the *Daily News*, but he was not the Zodiac.

British writer Colin Wilson published a book called *Order of the Assassins: The Psychology of Murder*, with a brief section on the Zodiac crimes that erroneously stated that ballistics comparisons proved the Zodiac used the same weapon in two attacks. *Chronicle* reporter Duffy Jennings included a chapter about the Zodiac in his 1974 collection of true crime stories titled *Great Crimes of San Francisco*. Jennings noted the Zodiac imposter "Sam" called the home of attorney Melvin Belli and was identified as a patient in a mental hospital.

In April 1974, a *Vallejo Times-Herald* story written by reporter Dave Peterson linked the Zodiac to the occult, witchcraft, and other unsolved murders. Sonoma County detective Erwin "Butch" Carlstedt believed the Zodiac was "tracing out a huge 'Z' on a map of the west" by killing several women in Washington state. News reports attributed the crimes to a man known as "Ted," who wore a sling on his arm to gain sympathy and lured his victims to their deaths. Carlstedt's theory fell apart in October 1975 with the arrest of a 28-year-old law student named Theodore Robert Bundy. Initially charged for attempted kidnapping, Ted Bundy was later exposed as one of the most prolific serial killers in American history, but he was not the Zodiac.

Another article by Dave Peterson referred to a man later known as the infamous "prime suspect" in the Zodiac investigation. "A Sonoma County man recently was considered a Zodiac suspect but was ruled out, according to Sonoma sheriff's captain Jim Caulder, head of investigations." Peterson described the individual as "a molester of young boys" who was "committed to Atascadero State Hospital." The suspect was Arthur Leigh Allen. He was convicted of molesting a young boy and began his sentence at Atascadero in March 1975. Department of Justice agents Jim Silver and Mel Nicolai believed Allen may have been responsible for the murders of young women in the Santa Rosa area, but they found no evidence linking him to those crimes. Allen submitted to a polygraph examination and the results indicated he was telling the truth when he denied any involvement in the Zodiac crimes and the Santa Rosa murders. Some people claimed Allen used drugs to pass the test, but polygraph examiners were trained to recognize any attempt to manipulate the results. Allen apparently hoped the lie-detector test would exonerate him, and he forged a letter using Agent Silver's name, which falsely claimed the DOJ had cleared Allen as a Zodiac suspect.

The shadow returns

SFPD inspectors Bill Armstrong and Dave Toschi had been hunting the Zodiac for years. Nicknamed "the Zodiac twins," the duo worked together on other high-profile cases, including the "Zebra killers," a group of black Muslims terrorists who targeted white victims in the San Francisco Bay Area for 179 days. The partnership ended in the summer of 1976 when Armstrong transferred to the Bunco fraud division to chase con men instead of murderers. Toschi remained the only investigator still assigned to the Zodiac case, and he liked playing the role of a celebrity cop. In his book *The Zebra Murders*, SFPD Inspector Earl Sanders described Toschi as likable and intelligent, but everyone knew "he had a thing about seeing his name in the paper," which caused problems.

On August 26, the *Chronicle* published a story about Toschi's pursuit of the killer. "I feel he's still out there," he said. "I feel he's going to surface." Toschi filled eight filing cabinet drawers with case files and information about 2,000 potential suspects. He admitted the investigation was "more personal" after Armstrong's departure, but he was trying "like hell" to catch the Zodiac. Unfortunately, most tips came from "mystics" and "eccentrics." Toschi often conferred with *Chronicle* cartoonist Robert Graysmith, who had developed his own obsession with the unsolved mystery. The inspector allowed Graysmith to view the actual Zodiac letters and other evidence.

Toschi also shared information regarding his "prime suspect," Arthur Leigh Allen. In August 1977, Allen was released from the psychiatric hospital in Atascadero. The convicted child molester reportedly sent Toschi a note which read, "I'm sorry I wasn't your man." Graysmith wrote that he heard about Allen's message and immediately said, "He's the one." Convinced Allen was the Zodiac, the cartoonist started his own amateur investigation. He followed Allen and created a plan to steal samples of the suspect's handwriting by forging copies and substituting them for the originals. Toschi had moved on to other suspects in the years since police found no evidence linking Allen to the Zodiac crimes. His public comments indicated he did not believe Allen was a good suspect. In January 1978, *San Francisco Examiner* reporter Tim Reiterman interviewed Toschi, who said police had fingerprints from the Stine murder scene and from a Napa telephone booth used by the Zodiac to make a positive identification. The fingerprints did not match Arthur Leigh Allen.

On April 24, 1978, someone sent an envelope to the *Chronicle*, postmarked somewhere in San Mateo County or in the Santa Clara area with two 13-cent stamps of the Liberty Bell. The accompanying

Robert Graysmith

letter written in blue ink looked somewhat similar to the previous Zodiac communications, with one distinct difference; the first line was indented.

> Dear Editor This is the Zodiac speaking I am back with you. Tell herb caen I am here, I have always been here. That city pig toschi is good but I am bu [crossed out] smarter and better he will get tired then leave me alone. I am waiting for a good movie about me. Who will play me. I am now in control of all things. yours truly: [crossed-circle] - guess SFPD - 0

Herb Caen wrote a daily column for the *Chronicle* and was a Bay Area legend. The Zodiac writer mentioned Dave Toschi, the first time a Zodiac letter referred to an investigator by name. In previous letters, the Zodiac expressed his hatred for the San Francisco police, but the writer of the new message uncharacteristically complimented Toschi. The letter also called Toschi a "city pig," as if to suggest the writer did not live in the city.

Handwriting expert Sherwood Morrill had retired but still served as a consultant on the case. He examined the new letter and concluded the Zodiac was the author. Inspector John Shimoda of the United States postal service crime lab also believed the new letter was authentic.

The return of the Zodiac dominated the headlines as investigators struggled to respond to the unexpected turn of events. The new message focused media attention and public pressure on Toschi and the department. Deputy Police Chief Clem DeAmicis assigned inspectors James Deasy and James Tedesco to assist Toschi, but he was no longer in charge of the case. The celebrity cop had become a liability and the Zodiac's return was a constant reminder of the inspector's failure to catch the killer.

Toschi contacted Graysmith about a new production of the musical, *The Mikado*. He told the cartoonist to watch the mail for a letter from the Zodiac. On May 2, someone who claimed to be the Zodiac sent a letter to the KHJ television station in Los Angeles.

Dear Channel Nine; This is the Zodiac speaking. You people in LA are in for a treat. In the next three weeks you are finally gona have something good to report. I have decided to begin killing again– PLEASE hold the applause! Nothing is going to happen until I do. You people just won't let me have it any other way. I plan to kill five people in the next three weeks. (1) Chief piggy Darrel Gates (2) Ex Chief piggy Ed Davis (3) Pat Boone – his theocratic crap is a obscenity to the rest of the world! (4) Also Eldrige Cleaver... And Susan Atkins – The Judas of the Manson Family. Shes gona get hers now. Hey - - - you actors - this is your lucky Break. Remember– whoever plays me has his work cut out for him. See you in the news.

Daryl Gates and Ed Davis both served as chief of the Los Angeles Police Department. Pat Boone was a popular singer known for his conservative Christian views. Eldridge Cleaver was a writer, political activist, and leader in the Black Panther movement. Susan Atkins was a devoted member of "The Family," a group of young dropouts led by the egomaniacal ex-convict Charles Manson. Acting on his instructions, Manson's followers murdered nine people in 1969. Atkins confessed but remained loyal to Manson until she became a born-again Christian and published a book called *Child of Satan, Child of God*.

The writer of the Channel Nine letter echoed the text of the April message and speculated about actors portraying the Zodiac in a movie. The first line of the new letter was indented and the handwriting was noticeably different than the original Zodiac communications. Authorities were skeptical and the possibility of forgery raised more questions about other messages attributed to the killer.

Cop scandal

Writer Armistead Maupin's long-running series in the *Chronicle* newspaper titled *Tales of the City* included a Zodiac-inspired storyline about a fictional killer known as "Tinkerbell." Dave Toschi appeared as a recurring character and consulted with the fictional SFPD inspector Henry Tandy, who "sent notes to himself from Tinkerbell" and was finally exposed as the real killer. The plot was intended to signal the writer's suspicion that Toschi was responsible for fan mail encouraging Maupin to continue featuring the real inspector in his series. Maupin learned that Herb Caen also received "phony fan mail," praising mention of Toschi in his column. Caen's assistant believed Toschi wrote the fan mail, and Maupin began to wonder if the inspector might have written the Zodiac letter that mentioned him by name.

Maupin contacted SFPD sergeant Jack O'Shea of the Police Intelligence Bureau to report his suspicions. US postal inspector John Shimoda was then asked to review the Zodiac letters, including the Riverside writings attributed to the killer by Sherwood Morrill. Shimoda concluded the Riverside messages were not written by the Zodiac. He initially agreed with Morrill and deemed the April letter authentic, but the expert later changed his mind and believed the letter was a forgery. Robert Prouty, chief of the Questioned Documents Section of the State Bureau of Criminal Identification and Investigation, also concluded the letter was not written by the Zodiac. Keith Woodward, former head of the documents department at the Los Angeles Police Department, believed the April letter was "a carefully drawn copy of the true Zodiac printing." Prouty said, "The general overall construction in the questioned documents indicates the letter was constructed by a person that had access to printed letters of Zodiac." CI&I documents examiner Terrence Pasco also concluded the April letter was a forgery. Morrill stood firm in his belief the letter was authentic and he criticized the other experts who contradicted his findings.

SFPD chief Charles Gain was troubled by the handwriting analysis and questioned Toschi, who admitted he had written the fan mail to

Maupin but denied forging any Zodiac letters. On July 11, 1978, Gain removed Toschi from the case and transferred him to the pawn shop detail. The chief told reporters there were doubts about the April letter, and some speculated about a possible connection between the forgery and the timing of Toschi's removal. Toschi was emotionally exhausted and went on sick leave, but the department later denied payment for his disability claims. Chief Gain finally announced the investigation had found no evidence that Toschi had forged the April letter, and added, "Anyone who had access to Zodiac material could have written the letter."

Dave Toschi denied the accusations of forgery and he was shocked when some observers suggested he might be the Zodiac killer. The so-called "Toschi scandal" effectively ended his career in the homicide division and his reputation never fully recovered after the public humiliation. Years later, some veteran SFPD investigators claimed Toschi had written some of the suspected Zodiac communications. One FBI report, dated August 16, 1979, stated, "Police chief Charles Gain, San Francisco, California Police Department has announced that Inspector David Toschi had actually written three letters himself to gain publicity for the Zodiac case." Gain may have stated Toschi wrote three of the fan letters to Armistead Maupin and the poorly worded description in the FBI report left the impression Gain said Toschi wrote three Zodiac letters. The San Francisco police department never issued any public statements linking Toschi to any specific Zodiac messages. Toschi repeatedly denied forging any Zodiac letters, but the cloud of suspicion followed him long after he eventually returned to duty in the robbery division.

Robert Graysmith lost his access to the SFPD files when Toschi was removed from the case, but he continued his amateur investigation.

In 1979, Graysmith claimed he had solved the Zodiac's 340-symbol cipher. Members of the American Cryptogram Association confirmed Graysmith's solution, but FBI experts concluded the cartoonist's deciphering was "forced" and "not a valid decryption." The FBI report further stated, "Just about any random selection of words could be arranged to be as 'logical'... When a cryptogram has been decrypted properly, there is an unmistakable sense of rightness about the solution. This sense of rightness is completely absent in the proposed solution." Like the Zodiac forgery in April 1978, Graysmith's solution included references to Herb Caen and "Toschi the pig."

In March 1981, someone mailed a letter to a television station in Atlanta, Georgia, where the unsolved murders of more than 20 black children had been dominating headlines since the summer of 1979.

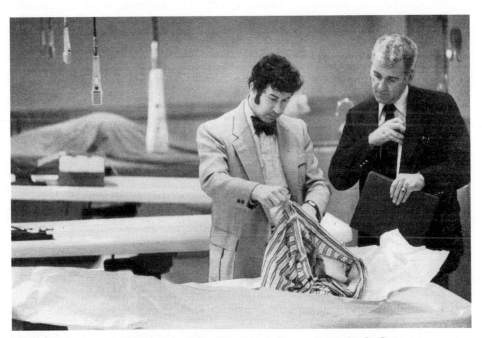

David Toschi and William Armstrong examine a victim's clothes, 29 March 1974.

The writer claimed to be the Zodiac and implied he was responsible for the child murders. Authorities did not believe the Zodiac was connected to the Atlanta crimes and 23-year-old Wayne Williams was later convicted of killing two adults with evidence prosecutors argued connected him to some of the child victims.

Making of a myth

The San Francisco Chronicle published an article titled *"One Killing Zodiac Might Have Planned Carefully,"* featuring a collection of stories about victim Darlene Ferrin. Reporter Bill Wallace relied on "a variety of sources" like Darlene's sisters Pam and Linda as well as a former babysitter named Karen, who all told stories they did not share with police during the original investigation years earlier. Karen claimed a mysterious man stalked Darlene shortly before she was killed. Darlene allegedly said the man was watching her because she had seen him kill someone. According to the article, a man who matched the same description reportedly bothered Darlene at the restaurant where she worked and he was also at a party in her apartment several months before the murder. Wallace wrote that the killer may have lured Darlene with a phone call just before she was killed and someone also made anonymous harassing calls to Darlene's friends and relatives "only minutes after she was murdered."

The babysitter waited until 1977 to share the seemingly important information about Darlene witnessing a murder and being stalked by the killer. Darlene's sister, Linda, had already identified a man named William Joseph Grant as the person who bothered Darlene at work, but investigators cleared him as a suspect. There was no evidence of any call luring Darlene before the murder and none of her friends reported suspicious telephone calls minutes after she was killed.

Dean Ferrin and his parents received anonymous telephone calls approximately ninety minutes after the shooting, but police did not believe the calls were made by the killer. The story about the stalker at Darlene's party was a new addition to the myths surrounding her death and became a central component in theories that she knew the Zodiac killer and was silenced to prevent her from revealing his identity.

The new stories about Darlene's murder expanded on storylines in the 1971 movie, *The Zodiac Killer*, and the 1979 book of the same name written by Jerry Weissman. In the movie, the Zodiac hangs out at a coffee shop and watches a waitress. In the book, the killer targets a young waitress because he believes she is a promiscuous whore. In the revisionist retellings, the connection between Darlene and the killer was the key element to unlock the entire Zodiac mystery. Most of these stories came from members of Darlene's family. Darlene's mother claimed her daughter said, "You might read about me in the newspapers tomorrow," on the night she was killed. Darlene's sister Pam claimed surviving victim, Michael Mageau, told Darlene's cousin, Sue Ayers, that the Zodiac mentioned Darlene's nickname "Dee" just before the murder. Sue said Michael never told her that story and also denied she ever told that story to Pam. Over the years, Pam claimed Darlene knew victim Betty Lou Jensen and witnessed the murder of Riverside victim Cheri Jo Bates. Darlene's husband, Dean, was disturbed by Pam's ongoing antics and advised others to discount her tall tales.

Book of shadows

The popular fiction about the life and death of Darlene Ferrin culminated in Robert Graysmith's 1986 book *Zodiac*. United Press

International writer Richard Harnett exposed the problem with Graysmith's version of the Zodiac story. Harnett wrote that a good account of all the facts in the Zodiac affair would have been a valuable contribution to local history, but Graysmith acted as an amateur sleuth rather than a historian. Harnett noted that Graysmith's book focused on his personal search for the Zodiac and the cartoonist neglected facts which did not fit into his scenario.

Some people involved in the case were critical of Graysmith's account, which included many inaccuracies and factual errors. SFPD officer Don Fouke described the book as "fiction." Armond Pelissetti, the first SFPD officer to arrive at the San Francisco crime scene, referred to Graysmith's account as "bullshit." Napa investigator Ken Narlow noted the cartoonist's placement of the Berryessa crime scene was incorrect. Graysmith incorrectly identified the locations of three Zodiac crime scenes and the payphone used to call police after the shooting in Vallejo. The book also repeated the myth that victim Cecelia Shepard had been stabbed 24 times to form the crossed-circle sign of the Zodiac. Graysmith wrote that the Zodiac's call to police was recorded, apparently based on statements by Darlene's sister, Pam, and former Vallejo police officer, Steve Baldino, who both claimed they had listened to the audio recording of the call. Police dispatcher Nancy Slover stated the Zodiac call was not recorded as the department did not have the equipment to record incoming calls in 1969.

Graysmith's book collected different stories about Darlene Ferrin into a narrative about a menacing stalker lurking in the shadows of her mysterious life. In the introduction of *Zodiac*, Graysmith told readers that one of the victims was murdered while "in the act of turning Zodiac in to police," an obvious reference to Darlene. The book also included the story about the killer chasing Darlene to the crime scene and calling out her nickname "Dee." Graysmith claimed a witness reported seeing a waitress arguing with a man outside Darlene's place of work on the night she was killed. According to police reports, the witness actually said the waitress and the man were not arguing but appeared to be talking about a car. The description of the waitress did not match Darlene, and the sighting occurred during the afternoon. Other stories about a stalker apparently combined incidents involving Darlene's rejected suitor, George, and William Joseph Grant. Graysmith's book named Grant as a suspect using the pseudonym "Andrew Todd Walker."

Other fictional elements converged in one story about a "painting party" at Darlene's home in May 1969. According to Graysmith, the guests included Darlene's younger brother, Leo, her sisters Pam and Linda, surviving victim, Michael Mageau, and his twin brother Stephen, a bartender named Paul, Vallejo police officers Buzz Gordon, Richard Hoffman, and Steve Baldino, and others. Darlene and Gordon reportedly had an affair and Hoffman was one of the first officers to arrive at the scene of the shooting at Blue Rock Springs. Hoffman stated that he did not attend the party.

Pam said Darlene was terrified by a sinister guest referred to as "Bob" in Graysmith's book and described as well-dressed, wearing dark-rimmed glasses, approximately 5ft 8in tall, 28 to 30 years old, with dark, curly, wavy hair. In this story, the man questioned Darlene about her sources of income and she was visibly upset in his presence. Linda identified William Joseph Grant as the stalker, but Pam said he was not the man at the party. Eventually, Darlene's sisters collectively identified six different men as the same stalker.

The story of the painting party first surfaced in 1977 when police interviewed Pam, Linda, and Darlene's babysitter, Karen. In a report,

Lt. Larry Haynes of the Concord Police Department wrote, "In regard to the painting party which took place in May of 1969 at 1300 Virginia, the new residence of Darlene Ferrin, it was determined that [Karen] was, in fact, there taking care of Darlene Ferrin's [daughter] and that the three unidentified white males arrived, and that she soon left the residence, due to the fact she was uncomfortable with these strange individuals. It's not certain whether any of these individuals may or may not have been the suspect. She did indicate that they were young." The report did not name the three males, but the three youngest men on Graysmith's list of guests were Darlene's younger brother, Leo, and the Mageau twins. Karen did not mention any other guests or the sinister stranger, and she did not stay for the party. After the publication of Graysmith's book, many other people claimed they were at the party along with numerous individuals accused of being suspects. Dean Ferrin denied stories about the party and said Darlene only invited a few friends to their home for a small get-together quite unlike the event described by others.

The list of party guests in Graysmith's book also included the name "Ron Allen," the brother of the cartoonist's prime suspect, Arthur Leigh Allen. In his book, Graysmith referred to Allen by the pseudonym "Bob Hall Starr," but he did not mention the name of the suspect's brother. Ron Allen said he did not attend this or any other party at the Ferrin home and he did not know Darlene, Dean, or any of the other people named as guests.

Graysmith wrote that Allen's family began to suspect he was the Zodiac in 1971, held a meeting to discuss their suspicions, and then decided to call SFPD inspector Dave Toschi. Police reports proved that Allen's family was surprised to hear he was considered a suspect. They never held such a meeting, they never called Toschi, and they did not believe Allen was the Zodiac. Graysmith told readers that Allen's father died in 1966, shortly before the Zodiac attacks began, and the death may have triggered the murders. Graysmith also speculated that Allen may have been wearing his father's clothes during the crimes. Allen's father, Ethan, died in 1971, long after the last-known Zodiac murder in 1969. Graysmith wrote that Allen's sister-in-law, Karen, said he spoke of man as true game, saw him holding papers with Zodiac-like symbols, and found bloody knives on the seat of his car. Karen denied these claims and explained Allen had a piece of paper with symbols that were not similar to the Zodiac writings or ciphers. Karen said Allen did not talk about "true game" and she did not see knives in his car. Police reports stated Allen was the one who mentioned bloody knives on his car seat during his 1971 interview with investigators.

In his book, Graysmith theorized Allen may have used a friend's car during the shooting at Blue Rock Springs Park in July 1969. Graysmith stated the car was at the station for repairs. According to police reports, Philip Tucker parked his Corvair at the station with a "For Sale" sign sometime in the summer of 1969. In 1971, Tucker told police Allen had never driven the Corvair. Allen worked at the gas station and Graysmith speculated he had access to Tucker's keys, but the owner fired Allen in April. Police determined the car was at the station for approximately two weeks in the summer, but Tucker and the owner could not remember the exact dates, so the car might not have been there on the night of the murder.

Handwriting analysis repeatedly excluded Allen as the author of the Zodiac letters, but Graysmith created an elaborate theory to explain how the killer fooled the experts. Graysmith believed the Zodiac used a projector to trace samples of handwriting from several different individuals. The resulting message combined the characteristics of multiple writers into the Zodiac's distinct style. In his book, Graysmith claimed documents examiner Sherwood Morrill confirmed the projector theory, but the retired expert consistently stated his certainty that the Zodiac produced the letters using his natural handwriting. The projector theory was further complicated by the Zodiac's handwritten message on the door of a victim's car at Lake Berryessa. A projector worked in darkness and required electricity, but the message was written during daylight in a remote area.

The fictional case against Allen might have seemed compelling to some readers, but, in an interview with a television producer, SFPD inspector Bill Armstrong denounced Graysmith's revisionist account as "hogwash." The book transformed the real-life Arthur Leigh Allen into the villain of the piece, the distorted character of Bob Hall Starr. Allen was forever marked by the book's portrayal of him and he could not escape the shadow of his doppelganger. Graysmith later wrote that many people learned of Allen's identity as a secret Zodiac suspect and his name was already circulating in rumors by October 1987.

Despite its many factual errors, exaggerations, and questionable claims, Graysmith's book was referred to as the "definitive" history of the unsolved mystery. Some members of the Vallejo Police Department reportedly relied on the book to learn the facts of the case. Journalists, crime buffs, amateur sleuths, and others accepted and repeated Graysmith's versions of events as fact. Renewed interest in the story generated more media coverage, which far too often relied on Graysmith's narrative as source material. The resulting misinformation clouded public perception and the popular myth became the true story.

In his review of *Zodiac*, writer Richard Harnett expressed concern that Graysmith's book "might even spur a 'Zodiac' to write to the newspapers again." Harnett's fears proved prophetic in October 1987 when a letter arrived at the offices of the *Vallejo Times-Herald*.

"This is the Zodiac speaking... Tell herb caen that I am still here. I have always been here... I will be out driving around on Halloween in my death machine looking for some kiddies to run over... Just like in the movie The car... Tell [crossed out] Toschi my new plans." The letter was signed, "Yours Truly: [crossed-circle] - guess VPD - 0."

Authorities did not believe the letter was authentic. The writer echoed the themes of the Zodiac forgery in April 1978 with references to a "movie," *Chronicle* columnist Herb Caen, and Inspector Dave Toschi, as well as the repetition of the words, "I am still here. I have always been here." The Zodiac threatened to kill "kiddies" with an explosive device he called "the death machine," but the new letter used that phrase to describe a vehicle. The 1977 horror movie, *The Car*, featured actor James Brolin as a sheriff battling a murderous 1971 Lincoln Continental apparently possessed by an evil spirit.

Zodiac II

The Zodiac mystery was featured in the 1989 documentary series *Crimes of the Century* with Mike Connors, star of the classic detective show *Mannix*. *Chronicle* reporter Paul Avery appeared with Vallejo police detective George Bawart, Napa investigator Ken Narlow, SFPD Officer Don Fouke, and Robert Graysmith. Avery recounted the story of a suspect reported by members of the Church of Satan.

Fouke again denied he had stopped the Zodiac killer on the night of the murder in San Francisco. The syndicated nationwide broadcast was the first extended television presentation about the case.

In November 1990, a man responsible for a series of shootings in New York sent a letter to the 17th police precinct on the east side of midtown Manhattan. The message began with the phrase, "This is the Zodiac," and seemed to suggest the killer selected his victims according to their astrological signs. Police and reporters were skeptical, so the writer sent another message to the *New York Post* that read, "One of the same Zodiac one Zodiac In San Francisco killed a man in the park with a gun and killed a woman with a knife and killed a man in the taxi cab with a gun." A small drawing of the Zodiac's hooded costume was followed by the words, "Me in the park is this similar no One Zodiac."

Eyewitness descriptions of the gunman proved he could not be the Zodiac and the imposter soon became known as "Zodiac II" or "Son of Zodiac." *New York Post* writer Kieran Crowley quickly realized the New York copycat used Graysmith's book "as a guide." *New York Daily News* columnist Mike McAlary wrote that the Son of Zodiac had obviously read Graysmith's book from cover to cover and added, "Beware... We live in the age of bad sequels." Several years later, in June 1996, police finally arrested 29-year-old Heriberto "Eddie" Seda after he shot his sister in the back. An unemployed high school dropout with a record of emotional problems and violence, Seda confessed and admitted he was inspired to imitate the Zodiac after reading Graysmith's book.

In December 1990, someone in Eureka, California mailed a red envelope to the *S.F. Chronicle*, which contained a greeting card featuring a snowman wearing a Groucho Marx mustache, nose, and glasses. The message read, "From your secret pal. Can't guess who I am yet? Well, look inside and you'll find out..." Inside, the text continued, "...That I'm gonna keep you guessin! Happy Holidays, anyway."

The card was accompanied by a photocopy of two US Postal Service keys for a post office box, but this apparent clue produced no viable leads. *Chronicle* employees did not recognize the card as a possible Zodiac communication, so the envelope was placed in a file folder and forgotten. In 2007, forensic documents examiner Lloyd Cunningham concluded the writing on the envelope did not match the Zodiac's writing. Cunningham did not conduct any proper handwriting comparisons and instead relied on his memory of the Zodiac's writing to reach his conclusion. A forger might have decided to exploit the opportunity created by the ongoing publicity surrounding the copycat killer in New York, or the real Zodiac quietly reasserted himself when the imposter threatened to steal the spotlight.

Primed suspect

While the New York copycat kept the "Zodiac" name in the headlines, an informant surfaced to accuse a ghost from the past. Fifty-year-old Ralph Spinelli, a career criminal with alleged ties to the Mafia, had been arrested on nine counts of armed robbery and sat in a cell at the Santa Clara county jail. He contacted police with an offer to reveal the identity of the Zodiac in exchange for a deal to avoid spending the rest of his life in prison. In June 1958, Spinelli and others were involved in a fight which resulted in the arrest of Arthur Leigh Allen. The charges were dismissed, but the animosity remained between Allen and Spinelli. In December 1990, Spinelli told police that a man came to him in late 1969 and asked for a job as a hitman. According to Spinelli, the man claimed to be the Zodiac and offered to kill a cabdriver in San Francisco shortly before the Zodiac killed cabdriver Paul Stine. Spinelli insisted that all charges against him be dropped before he identified the man as Arthur Leigh Allen.

Vallejo police captain Roy Conway and retired detective George Bawart launched a new investigation. Allen worked at the Ace Hardware store in Vallejo and lived alone in the house on Fresno Street after his mother's death in October 1989. In February 1991, police searched Allen's home and found several guns, pipe bombs, and "sadistic-type pornography," including an audio recording of Allen "spanking a young boy who was feigning pain." None of the weapons could be linked to Zodiac crimes. The pipe bombs were not similar to the Zodiac's explosive devices, although a handwritten formula found in Allen's home was described as similar to the commonplace ingredients of bombs as detailed in Zodiac letters. The search did not yield any new evidence, but the police activity attracted attention and reporters soon revealed Allen's identity as a Zodiac suspect in May 1991. In an interview with *Vallejo Times-Herald* writer Jacqueline Ginley, SFPD inspector Dave Toschi "declined to discuss why Allen was dismissed as a suspect" after the investigation in the early 1970s. Allen told Ginley that he was not responsible for the Zodiac crimes and denied Spinelli's claims. The suspect complained that he had been haunted by the Zodiac accusations for two decades and considered contacting famed attorney Melvin Belli for help, but he did not believe police would find any evidence to justify further investigation.

On August 16, 1991, George Bawart met with surviving victim Michael Mageau at the airport in Ontario, California. He hoped Mageau could identify Allen as the shooter at Blue Rock Springs Park on July 4, 1969. Bawart displayed photographs of six individuals, including Arthur Leigh Allen. Mageau reportedly pointed to Allen's photograph and said, "That's him." According to Vallejo police captain Joann West, Mageau said he was "pretty sure" about his identification, but then said the shooter had a "round face like that of another individual that was in the line-up." Mageau rated his certainty as an 8 on a scale of 1 to 10. Police considered Mageau's conflicting identification unreliable at best. In 1969, Allen did not match the physical description of the shooter provided by Mageau, who admitted he had only seen the departing killer briefly in a profile view. District Attorney Mike Nail doubted that Allen would be charged and told reporters, "I really suspect that nothing's going to come of it." VPD Chief Gerald Galvin said he did not expect Allen would be arrested. Allen repeated his claims of innocence in television interviews and famously declared, "I'm not the damn Zodiac."

The unsolved mystery was featured on many of the tabloid TV shows popular in the 1990s, including a series hosted by Geraldo Rivera, known for his disastrous live television event opening the empty vault of legendary gangster Al Capone. Rivera's 1988 TV special, *Exposing Satan's Underground*, scared away advertisers but attracted millions of viewers by exploiting what became known as "the satanic panic," the paranoid hysteria resulting from years of baseless conspiracy theories about devil-worshipping cults engaged in ritual child abuse across America. *Washington Post* writer Tom Shales criticized the NBC network for broadcasting two hours of "butchered babies, dismembered corpses, cannibal cults, and sex orgies." The special featured writer Maury Terry, known for his theories linking the Son of Sam shootings in New York, the Manson murders, and many other crimes to a worldwide network of satanists. In 1991, Rivera launched a syndicated show titled *Now It Can Be Told* with a new "investigation" of the Zodiac crimes. Rivera and Terry quickly concluded that a satanic cult was probably behind the Zodiac murders. The show rehashed many of the ever-changing stories about victim Darlene Ferrin and suggested she was somehow involved in the occult. Her sister, Pam, said Darlene gave the killer the name Zodiac. In another episode of *Now It Can Be Told*, Pam confronted victim Michael Mageau in a hidden-camera segment titled "*The Man Who Knew Too Much.*" Pam questioned Michael and cried out, "I know you know who did it! I know you do!" Michael seemed stunned by Pam's sudden arrival and the accusations. He quietly replied, "I don't know. I can't remember a lot of those names."

Pam was interviewed in many other television shows, but her appearance on a daytime talk series with Sally Jessy Raphael stunned the audience, the guests, and even the host. Pam expanded the story about Darlene's seemingly prophetic statements. "Well, the night that she was killed... she had told my mom, 'Remember that killing I told you about a few years ago, well, it's gonna be in the papers tomorrow so don't be surprised.'" Pam said she was tormented by an anonymous stalker who she believed was the Zodiac killer. "I believe that the man that killed her is the man that killed Cheri Jo Bates also, which is the stabbing that she seen—she seen her get killed—she knew Cheri Jo... And when it got down to when he killed Betty Lou, which was a girl that Darlene used to babysit for– her parents say she didn't, but I believe that she did, she knew Betty Lou." Guests Robert Graysmith and psychologist James Alan Fox watched in disbelief as Pam explained that the evidence which could prove her claims had been stolen by a man who broke into her home and knocked her unconscious just before the show.

On August 26, 1992, Arthur Leigh Allen died from apparent complications of diabetic kidney failure. Vallejo police once again searched his home but found nothing connecting him to the Zodiac crimes. A draft of an agreement submitting to another polygraph examination was in the suspect's printer. Investigators were initially excited by the discovery of a VHS tape marked "Z," which reportedly included recordings of TV news reports about the Zodiac case. In April 1993, VPD captain Roy Conway, retired detective George Bawart, and Robert Graysmith appeared at a conference on the campus of San Francisco State University. They all agreed that Allen was most likely the Zodiac. Conway later said that he would have filed charges if Allen were still alive; however, any attempt to prosecute Allen for the murder of Darlene Ferrin would most likely have failed. The evidence was insufficient and most prosecutors would not rely on the questionable identification of the suspect by victim Michael Mageau. Experts concluded that Allen did not write the Zodiac letters and defense attorneys could argue an alternative theory of the crime in which the real Zodiac killer was responsible for the murder. Conway and others may have been eager to close the case, but Allen's death left the mystery unsolved and other suspects were readily available to replace him.

A 1996 episode of the TV show, *Hard Copy*, featured Harvey Hines, a former Escalon police officer, who was convinced he had identified the Zodiac as a man named Larry Kane. Hines believed Kane abducted and killed Donna Lass, the nurse who disappeared from the Lake Tahoe area in 1970 and became known as a possible Zodiac victim after a postcard attributed to the killer included a reference to Lake Tahoe. Another possible Zodiac victim, Kathleen Johns, identified Kane as the man she encountered on Highway 132 in March 1970. Police investigated and eventually cleared Kane as a suspect when handwriting and fingerprint comparisons indicated he was not the Zodiac.

Darkening shadows

In May 1997, a janitor in Kobe, Japan, discovered the severed head of a young boy with a message inside the victim's mouth signed, "Zodiac." In subsequent letters, the killer taunted police and explained his motives. "So this is the beginning of the game... I desperately want to see people die. Nothing makes me more excited than killing. Stupid police, stop me if you can. It's great fun for me to kill people... A bloody judgment is needed for my years of bitterness... It's only when I kill that I am liberated from the constant hatred that I suffer and that I am able to attain peace. It is only when I give pain to people that I can ease my own pain." The Kobe "Zodiac" murdered two children and wounded three others. Police arrested a 14-year-old boy with mental health problems who tortured and killed animals. He was released from prison in 2005 and published his autobiography in 2015.

The legend of the Zodiac continued to spread around the world with new internet message boards where members shared information, presented theories, and debated various aspects of the case. Curious crime buffs learned about the story on websites devoted to the mystery, and police reports, crime scene photographs, FBI files, and other materials were available to the public. New books introduced more suspects, including Ted Kaczynski, also known as "The Unabomber." The theory was featured in the popular series *Unsolved Mysteries,* while other television documentaries focused on familiar faces such as Arthur Leigh Allen and Larry Kane. *America's Most Wanted* included reenactments of the crimes and interviews with Kathleen Johns and codebreaker Don Harden. Journalist Bill Curtis also examined the Zodiac case in the television show *Cold Case Files* with SFPD officer Armond Pelissetti, VPD detective George Bawart, former Napa County sheriff's investigator Ken Narlow, retired DOJ agent Mel Nicolai, Robert Graysmith, and others.

SFPD Inspectors Mike Maloney and Kelly Carroll appeared in an episode of the ABC series *Primetime*, which focused on efforts to obtain DNA evidence from the stamps and envelopes sent by the Zodiac. Several items were tested, including the stamps on envelopes containing a Zodiac cipher and a piece of a victim's bloodstained shirt. Dr. Cynde Holt said she found the partial DNA profile of a male individual which was insufficient to positively identify anyone but might be used to eliminate suspects. The DNA did not match Arthur Leigh Allen or some of the other men named as suspects over the years. Critics cited problems with the methods used to obtain the partial profile and skeptics claimed the DNA belonged to postal workers, newspaper staff, police, or others who handled the Zodiac communications.

Handwriting experts concluded Allen did not write the Zodiac letters. SFPD officer Don Fouke reportedly said that Allen was not the man he saw near the scene of the Zodiac's last known murder in October 1969. The DNA evidence also indicated Allen was not the Zodiac, but Robert Graysmith continued his campaign to convict the suspect in the court of public opinion. During his appearance on the History Channel show *Perfect Crimes*, Graysmith claimed the Zodiac sent a new letter one day after Allen was released from prison. The letter in question was sent in April 1978 and Allen was released from prison in August 1977. In interviews for *Primetime, Ashley Banfield: On Location, The Abrams Report,* and *Larry King Live,* Graysmith repeatedly stated that Allen had known and stalked the Zodiac victims, could be placed at the crime scenes, and was reported to police by his own family.

The dust jacket of Graysmith's book about the Unabomber case referred to him as the man who solved the Zodiac mystery. Graysmith hoped to close the case with his sequel titled *Zodiac Unmasked: The Identity of America's Most Elusive Serial Killer Revealed.* Graysmith said the new book contained more than 500 pages of material cut from his first book. Once again, Graysmith relied heavily on stories from questionable sources, including Allen's estranged former friend, Don Cheney. In interviews with Graysmith and others, Cheney embellished his stories to further implicate Allen. He said Allen was wearing a new Zodiac wristwatch at the time of their last meeting. Cheney claimed that Allen had taken him to the crime scene on Lake Herman Road shortly after the murders in December 1968. He also said Allen took him to the Pancake House located near the home of Allen's parents and pointed out a young waitress Cheney later identified as Zodiac victim, Darlene Ferrin. Cheney echoed a story in Graysmith's first book about a mysterious, well-dressed stranger at a painting party in Darlene's home. Graysmith named Ron Allen as one of the party guests, and Cheney claimed Allen's brother, Ron, and his wife, Karen, attended such a party and told him Allen was also there dressed in a suit. Cheney also claimed Allen talked about killing many people in one attack by flying a plane into the Sears Tower. According to Cheney's timing of events, he last saw Allen in December 1968 or January 1969, but construction of the Sears Tower did not begin until August 1970. Cheney said Darlene's husband hired Allen to kill her and the husband was a powerful drug dealer in the Vallejo area. Cheney never mentioned these seemingly important details when he was interviewed by police decades earlier. VPD detective George Bawart eventually stated that Cheney was not a credible witness.

In *Zodiac Unmasked*, Graysmith referred to a telephone call to the home of lawyer Melvin Belli from someone who claimed to be the Zodiac and declared, "Today's my birthday!" FBI reports indicated the call occurred sometime in January 1970, but Graysmith dated the call on Allen's birthday, December 18, 1969. In real life, police identified the caller as the same Zodiac imposter who talked with Belli on the Jim Dunbar television show in October 1969. Graysmith also wrote that he discovered a "hidden" road, which led from Allen's Vallejo home to the Zodiac crime scenes, but area maps and a search of local geography proved the hidden road never existed.

Graysmith's books served as the basis for director David Fincher's 2007 film *Zodiac*, starring actor Jake Gyllenhall as the cartoonist. An early draft of the screenplay included a fictional ending, with Graysmith presenting his case against Allen to agents of the Department of Justice. The final film adjusted the facts to its original source material and focused largely on Graysmith's fictional relationship with *Chronicle* reporter Paul Avery. Graysmith's character becomes convinced that the Zodiac "birthday" call to Melvin Belli proves Arthur Leigh Allen was the killer. The movie ends with victim, Michael Mageau, identifying Allen and a title card informs viewers that the deceased child molester remains the prime suspect. *Zodiac* was a financial failure, but some critics praised the film as a compelling portrait of obsession. *San Francisco Chronicle* film critic, Mark LaSalle, described *Zodiac* as a "puzzle riddled with holes" that could only suggest an element of obsession most likely not based in reality. The film adaptation of Graysmith's version of the Zodiac story cemented popular myths and inspired a new wave of armchair detectives and imposters.

In June 2008, the body of a young, pregnant woman was found in a bathtub at the Fairfield Inn in Fayetteville, North Carolina. Twenty-three-year-old Megan Lynn Touma, a dental specialist at the Bragg military base, had been strangled and died of asphyxiation. The killer used lipstick to draw a large crossed-circle on the hotel mirror, and a local newspaper soon received a typed letter signed with the same symbol. "To whom it may concern. The following is to inform that I am responsible for the dead body that was found... It was a master piece. I confess, that I have killed many times before in several states, but now I will start using my model's signature. There will be many more to come. Fayetteville law enforcement are very incompetent. I basically sat there and watch while investigators were on site." Megan's fiancé, Sgt. Edgar Patino Lopez, later confessed and police found the typewriter used to produce the letter in his home. He served in the 18th Engineer Brigade and trained in psychological tactics for media propaganda.

The Zodiac case was one of the greatest unsolved mysteries in American history and the killer became a true crime legend. Like London's Jack the Ripper, the Zodiac was reinvented in books, movies, and television shows, while popular theories contended he was responsible for dozens of murders. The image of a prolific killer who lurked in the shadows behind many other unsolved crimes and evaded capture for decades transformed the Zodiac into a modern bogeyman.

CHAPTER 4:
THEORIES

*"I say a murder is abstract. You pull the trigger
and after that you do not understand
anything that happens."*
Jean-Paul Sartre

The Zodiac alluded to unknown victims and the box scores he often included in his letters indicated an increasing body count, but investigators could not definitively link the killer to any other unsolved crimes. In the letter sent to the *Los Angeles Times* in 1971, the writer seemed to take credit for the murder of Riverside City College student, Cheri Jo Bates, and the words, "there are a hell of a lot more down there," implied the Zodiac claimed other unidentified victims in Southern California.

In cold blood

In 2017, historian Kristi Hawthorne noticed an unsolved case contained similar elements to the Zodiac's last-known murder. On the night of April 9, 1962, an unidentified man called the police station in Oceanside, California, located on the Pacific Coast approximately 40 miles north of San Diego. The caller said, "I am going to pull something here in Oceanside and you will never be

able to figure it out." The following night, 29-year-old cab driver Ray Davis traveled downtown and then disappeared after reporting that he was taking a passenger to the southern part of the city. Hours later, police inspected the abandoned cab at the 400 block of South Pacific Street. Someone apparently sat in the back of the vehicle, fired one bullet at the windshield, and fired another bullet through the driver's seat. Blood stains showed the bullet hit someone sitting in the driver's seat, but the victim was not in the cab. On the passenger seat, police found a paperback copy of the crime novel *Dance With the Dead*, part of author Richard Prather's series of books featuring the popular character of private detective, Shell Scott. In the story, Scott investigates the murder of a friend with clues found in a men's magazine, revolving around 12 centerfolds representing each month of the calendar year.

A police officer discovered the body of Ray Davis in an alley behind the home of the former mayor, Joe McDonald, at 1926 South Pacific Street. At the time, mayor Erwin Sklar lived across the street. A gunshot wound in the victim's back corresponded to the bullet hole in the driver's seat of the cab, and another bullet had been fired into the back of his head. The murder weapon was a .22 caliber gun loaded with long rifle ammunition. The killer did not take the money in Ray's pockets.

After Davis was killed, Oceanside police received another telephone call from the anonymous man who said, "Do you remember me calling you last week and telling you that I was going to pull a real baffling crime? I killed the driver and I am going to get me a bus driver next." Information about the first call was withheld from the public and police concluded that the same man was responsible for the second call. Authorities scrambled to protect bus drivers, but the caller never acted on his threat. The killing apparently stopped, police did not identify any viable suspects, and the case remained unsolved.

The Oceanside killer left the victim's body in the upscale residential neighborhood of St. Malo. The Zodiac murdered cab driver Paul Stine in the upscale residential neighborhood of Presidio Heights in San Francisco. After Stine was killed, the Zodiac threatened to attack a school bus and shoot the children. After Davis was killed, an anonymous caller threatened to kill a bus driver. Davis was shot with a .22 caliber weapon and two Zodiac victims were shot with a .22 caliber weapon. These similarities fueled speculation linking the Zodiac to the Davis murder, but other aspects of the cases were inconsistent. Unlike the Zodiac, the Oceanside killer transported and dumped the victim's body, and he also drove the victim's car after the murder. The Zodiac called police after his crimes, while the anonymous caller in Oceanside called police before and after the attack. Ray Davis may have been murdered by the Zodiac or another killer who randomly selected a cab driver as a victim.

Shoot to kill

On the afternoon of Sunday, June 2, 1963, a sniper fired shots at a group of teenage surfers in a secluded area near Gaviota State Park, approximately 30 miles northwest of Santa Barbara, California. No one was hurt and the gunman escaped. Seven miles east of the shooting scene, campers also reported hearing shots in the early morning hours. Sheriff's officers believed the sniper used a .22 caliber rifle, but no evidence was recovered at the scenes. The shootings seemed like random incidents until the bodies of a young couple were discovered between the two locations.

Eighteen-year-old Robert Domingos and his 17-year-old girlfriend Linda Edwards lived in Lompoc, California, and were engaged to be married. On June 4th, 1963, they took advantage of the high school "Senior Ditch Day" to relax on the beach at Cañada Del Molino. The evidence indicated Robert and Linda were confronted by a man holding a .22 caliber weapon loaded with Winchester Super X long rifle ammunition. He produced clothesline pre-cut in 3/8 inch-long segments and intended to bind the victims, but something apparently went wrong when Robert resisted and possibly fought with the attacker. The two teenagers tried to run away, but the man opened fire. Robert was shot 11 times and Linda was hit by nine bullets. Spent casings were ejected along a dry creek bed as the gunman chased the victims and shot them in the back. Autopsies revealed that some of the shots were fired after the victims had already fallen to the ground.

The killer dragged the bodies into a nearby wooden lean-to-shack and then discarded some clothesline and empty cartridge boxes inside. A lot number identified the cartridge boxes as ammunition available at the Vandenberg Air Force Base near Lompoc and other locations. At some point, the man used a knife to cut open the sides of Linda's one-piece bathing suit, but there were no signs of any sexual assault. He also slashed Linda's body in several places after she was dead. The killer apparently intended to destroy the evidence when he used matches to set the shack on fire, but he left the area and did not realize the flames died out shortly after his departure.

The case was still unsolved when the Santa Barbara County Sheriff's Office launched a new investigation in 1971. Detective Bill Baker of the Major Crimes Unit studied the files and reviewed the evidence. Elements of the Domingos/Edwards murders were similar to the Zodiac's attack at Lake Berryessa, including the pre-cut lengths of clothesline used to bind the victims and the selection of victims at a secluded location near water. A .22 caliber weapon and Super X long rifle ammunition were used in the Santa Barbara killings and the shooting on Lake Herman Road. Detective Baker met with Department of Justice agent Mel Nicolai and SFPD inspectors Dave Toschi and Bill Armstrong. The investigators agreed that the Zodiac was a logical suspect in the 1963 murders. Baker appeared at a press conference to address the possible Zodiac connection and the sheriff's office issued a statement, which read, "Considerable evidence points to the murders of Linda Edwards and Robert Domingos as being the work of the infamous Zodiac."

Baker and others speculated the Zodiac had learned from his mistakes in the Santa Barbara crime and adapted his methods for the attack at Lake Berryessa. Robert and Linda were most likely afraid the killer would hurt them, so they resisted and tried to escape. At Lake Berryessa, the killer told the victims that robbery was his motive and he would not hurt them. Convinced they were not in danger, the victims did not try to escape and instead allowed themselves to be bound with the pieces of clothesline. The killer then stabbed the victims once they were subdued and unable to escape. Robert and Linda were shot as they ran away and the attacker only used the knife after the victims were dead.

Months after the Santa Barbara murders, detectives wondered if the killer was responsible for another double murder in San Diego, California. Nineteen-year-old Johnny Ray Swindle and his wife Joyce Ann, 19, were married in Alabama on January 18, 1964 and traveled to San Diego to enjoy their honeymoon before he returned to duty on the Navy radar ship *Chevalier*. On the night of February 5, shortly after 8:00 p.m., Johnny and Joyce left their apartment at the Paradise Court and went to nearby Ocean Beach. The couple walked onto a patio at the rear of the Silver Spray Hotel surrounded by rocky cliffs and high bluffs. They could not see the sniper positioned on a cliff approximately 50 feet above the patio, armed with a .22 Remington rifle model 550-1 loaded with .22 caliber, long rifle, hollow-point bullets.

The gunman opened fire. A bullet hit Joyce in the upper left arm and continued into her chest. Another bullet hit Joyce on the left side of her back and damaged her spine. Johnny apparently moved to protect his wife and the sniper shot him. One bullet entered his upper left arm, then exited and continued into his left thigh. Another bullet penetrated the top of his head above the right eye. After Johnny and Joyce were incapacitated, the sniper came down from the cliff and walked over to his victims. He fired another bullet into Johnny's left ear at close range, leaving powder burns on the skin. The man took Johnny's wallet and shot Joyce in the back of the head.

Witnesses saw a man standing on the rocks around the time of the shooting and another man was seen running away from the area. Several suspects were investigated and cleared, including a local recluse and a marine who killed his family with an ax. Santa Barbara County sheriff's detectives traveled to San Diego with a bullet from the Domingos/Edwards case and ballistics experts concluded the Swindles were killed with a different gun. Days after the Zodiac murders on Lake Herman Road in December 1968, San Diego police chief O.J. Reid contacted the Solano County Sheriff's Office and submitted bullets from the Swindle case for ballistics comparison, but the analysis proved two different weapons were used in the crimes. Like the Santa Barbara case, the murders of Johnny and Joyce Swindle remained unsolved.

Decorated Vietnam veteran John Franklin Hood, 24, and his fiancée, Sandra Garcia, 20, were beaten and stabbed to death at East Beach in Santa Barbara on Saturday, February 21, 1970. Robbery was not a motive and there were no signs of any sexual assault. On July 4, 1970, three teenagers hitched a ride in a van with three other men and then decided to spend the night on a beach near Campus Point, approximately 11 miles west of the Hood/Garcia crime scene. According to news reports, the victims were in sleeping bags when someone attacked them with a "sharp instrument." Thomas Dolan and Homer Shadwick died, but Thomas Hayes survived. The evidence did not establish the crimes were connected and the cases were never solved. The three men in the van were investigated as potential suspects, but some theories named the Zodiac as the killer.

Missing links

The murder of Riverside City College student, Cheri Jo Bates, was often cited as a possible Zodiac crime, but local police dismissed any connection and focused on their prime suspect who had known the victim. Some theories proposed the Zodiac did not kill Bates but did write the "Confession" letter and notes sent to police, a local newspaper, and Cheri Jo's father. A Zodiac letter claimed responsibility for the failed abduction of Kathleen Johns in 1970, but skeptics questioned her story and claimed the Zodiac exploited the publicity and lied about his involvement.

A suspected Zodiac message, which mentioned Lake Tahoe and referred to "victim 12," was interpreted as a reference to the disappearance of 25-year-old nurse Donna Lass. On September 5,

1970, Donna worked a night shift at the Sahara Hotel and Casino resort near Lake Tahoe, Nevada and she signed out around 1:45 a.m. Donna's car was later found in the parking lot by her apartment, but she had disappeared. Some reports stated that an unidentified man called Donna's place of work and her landlord to report that she had to leave due to a family emergency. A report written by a private investigator hired by Donna's family cast doubt on the idea that the killer was responsible for the telephone calls and attributed the stories to confusion and miscommunication. Donna's sister, Mary Pilker, and other family members could not believe the young nurse walked away from her life and they were certain she had been abducted. Police had no leads and suspected Donna was most likely dead. The Zodiac postcard rekindled interest in Donna's case.

In December 1974, an envelope was delivered to Mary's home in Sioux Falls, South Dakota, which contained a greeting card featuring a snowy scene and pine trees. Inside, the card read, "Holiday Greetings and Best Wishes for a Happy New Year." The sender had written, "Best Wishes, St. Donna & Guardians of the Pines." The cursive writing was not similar to the Zodiac letters, but some people believed the greeting card was just another psychological attack by the elusive killer.

Napa County sheriff's detective Ken Narlow thought the Zodiac might have been responsible for a knife attack north of San Francisco on the night of Friday April 7, 1972. Thirty-three-year-old legal secretary Isobel Watson stepped off a bus in the Tamalpais Valley and walked on Pine Hill Road toward her home. A light-colored vehicle hit Isobel and knocked her onto the sidewalk. The driver stopped the car and apologized. He offered to give her a ride home, but she declined. The man insisted and said, "Please let me drive you home."

Isobel refused and the man suddenly produced a knife and stabbed her several times in her shoulder and neck. He then ran back to his car and drove away. Isobel was taken to a hospital and recovered. She said the driver was a white male in his forties, approximately 5ft 9in tall, with brown hair and dark-rimmed glasses. The details were similar to the descriptions of the man who killed San Francisco cab driver Paul Stine in October 1969 and the man who reportedly tried to abduct Kathleen Johns in March 1970. Isobel survived, but the attacker was never identified.

Robert Graysmith's book, *Zodiac*, included a list of 49 possible Zodiac victims. In some cases, the MO was remarkably different than the Zodiac crimes. The cause of death varied from shot, stabbed, strangled, beaten, drugs, exposure, to "unknown." Some of the women on the list were identified as victims in the unsolved murders of hitchhikers in Santa Rosa, California during the 1970s. Arthur Leigh Allen, the "prime suspect" in the Zodiac case, owned a trailer in Santa Rosa and was also investigated for the hitchhiker murders. Police examined other potential suspects, including prolific serial killer Ted Bundy and the cousins Angelo Buono and Kenneth Bianchi, known as the Hillside Stranglers. In August 1976, 41-year-old junior college instructor, Fredric Manalli, was killed in a head-on collision in Santa Rosa. Police searched Manalli's possessions and found a drawing, which reportedly depicted the sadistic murder of his former student, a hitchhiker victim named Kim Wendy Allen. The investigation did not produce any other evidence linking Manalli to the crimes and the Santa Rosa murders remained unsolved.

An anonymous letter claimed the Zodiac was linked to "the Atlanta child murders" in Georgia. The first victims were killed in 1979 and the total number of victims reached at least 20 children.

In March 1981, someone sent an envelope to the WXIA television station in Atlanta. The handwriting and letter formations were not similar to the Zodiac's style and the first line of the text was indented.

> "Hello it's me. Haven't you people figured out who is killed these little people yet. I'll give you a hint. I used to be in San Francisco. I used to stalk women, but I like to kill children now. At all my victims bodies I have left "certain clues, but I guess it's too much you Revels to handle. So I guess I'll have to tell you. I'll tr kill children because are so easy to "pick off: Buy the way, if you still have letters from the other murders, I am not writing in the same hand writing. Zodiac [crossed-circle]."

A crossed-circle was drawn on the upper left side of the envelope instead of a return address. In October 1969, the Zodiac had also drawn the symbol in the same place on the envelope mailed to the *S.F. Chronicle*, which contained a bloodstained piece of a victim's shirt. On his website Zodiacciphers.com, Richard Grinell argued the detail about the 1969 envelope was not known to the public in 1981 and the placement of the symbol therefore indicated the Atlanta letter was written by the Zodiac. An FBI memo stated handwriting analysts could not determine if the Zodiac had written the Atlanta letter, but the Bureau also recommended the Zodiac should not be eliminated as the author based on the available evidence and information at that time. Investigators did not believe the Zodiac was responsible for any of the child murders later attributed to Wayne Williams after his arrest in June 1981.

Various theories linked the Zodiac to many other infamous cases, including the murder of "Black Dahlia" Elizabeth Short in

Los Angeles, the Moonlight Murders by the "Phantom killer" in Texarkana, Arkansas, the B.T.K. strangler in Wichita, Kansas, the Chicago Tylenol killings, the murder of child beauty pageant star JonBenét Ramsey in Colorado, and the crimes of the "Golden State Killer," Joseph James DeAngelo.

Blood simple

The Zodiac was often portrayed as a prolific serial killer, but one theory proposed that he never existed. In this scenario, someone created the Zodiac letters as a hoax and took credit for random and unrelated crimes. A television show titled *The Myth of the Zodiac Killer* promoted the hoax theory but failed to substantiate its central claims or resolve problems with the no-Zodiac narrative. Three Zodiac letters were sent with pieces of the bloodstained shirt worn by victim Paul Stine and established a direct link between the writer and the killer. The hoax theory did not explain how the writer gained access to the victim's shirt, but suggested that a reporter or someone connected to the San Francisco Police Department had stolen the evidence. The man who stabbed the victims at Lake Berryessa left a message on a car door and the handwriting was similar to the Zodiac letters. Bootprints led from the crime scene to the car, establishing a direct link between the writer and the killer. *The Myth* show presented the conclusions of linguistic analysts who examined the language, word usage, and other aspects of the Zodiac messages, and speculated that the first Zodiac letters sent in July 1969 were not written by the same person, or persons, who sent all of the other suspected Zodiac communications. Two Zodiac letters contained quotations from the Gilbert and Sullivan musical, *The Mikado*, but the analysts did not mention how those portions of the text factored into their analysis and conclusions. The implausible hoax theory required at least four different killers, including a Zodiac copycat at Lake Berryessa, and two Zodiac forgers with similar handwriting who also possessed sufficient knowledge of codes and cryptography to construct the Zodiac ciphers.

According to other theories, the Zodiac was an evil genius who planted clues to his identity and motives in his letters and murdered innocent people as part of some elaborate plan. Sonoma County detective Erwin "Butch" Carlstedt believed the Zodiac created a giant "Z" on a map by killing several women. The Zodiac wrote that a map and his 32-symbol cipher "concerned radians and # inches along the radians." A radian is an angle of 57.3 degrees, defined as an angle subtended by an arc of a circle equal in length to the radius of a circle. Gareth Penn, a former reference librarian, examined a map of the Bay Area and then measured the angle formed by the peak of Mt. Diablo and two Zodiac crime scenes with a protractor. He believed the locations of the murders in Vallejo and San Francisco created a radian angle and the Zodiac combined geometry, geography, and murder into a work of conceptual art. Penn incorrectly identified a Vallejo golf course as the crime scene instead of the correct location across the street in Blue Rock Springs Park. The Zodiac apparently intended the map and cipher to help authorities find a specific location, but Blue Rock Springs Park was not visible on the killer's map. Penn focused on one radian and did not account for the Zodiac's instructions regarding multiple "radians." The actual angle formed by Mt. Diablo and the two crime scenes was not one radian at 57.3 degrees but instead measured 60 degrees or more. The Zodiac may have selected the locations of his attacks in a complex geometric design, but Penn's one radian theory was not valid. Penn published a book, *Times 17*, and declared he had identified the Zodiac as a Harvard lecturer.

In one popular conspiracy theory, Zodiac victim Darlene Ferrin was killed because she knew a dangerous secret and the other crimes were staged as the work of a madman to misdirect the investigation and conceal the true motive to silence her. Pam claimed her sister Darlene knew at least one Zodiac victim and witnessed a murder. Speculation expanded these scenarios to include connections between Darlene and all of the Zodiac victims via an illicit drug ring, a satanic cult, or some unknown association. The available evidence did not indicate a conspiracy or any link between the victims.

The unsolved case was left open to interpretation and many theories could seem compelling until the truth was finally revealed. Only the killer knew the answers, but more than a dozen law enforcement agencies failed to capture the Zodiac. Some people viewed the mystery as a challenge and launched their own amateur investigations. Those identified as possible suspects were forever marked as their names entered the history books.

CHAPTER 5:
THE ACCUSED

"Every murderer is probably somebody's old friend."
Agatha Christie

The Zodiac mystery was an irresistible riddle and countless amateur sleuths were driven to obsession in their quest to identify the killer. According to popular accounts, more than 2,500 men were investigated by police, but most of the individuals publicly named as suspects were originally accused by theorists who claimed they had solved the case. Former *San Francisco Chronicle* cartoonist Robert Graysmith and others were convinced that Arthur Leigh Allen was the Zodiac, although the evidence did not link him to the crimes. The list of alternative suspects included men plucked from obscurity as well as notorious criminals such as The Unabomber, Ted Kaczynski, and a member of Charles Manson's family of killers. A lawyer held a press conference and claimed his brother was the Zodiac, and fathers were accused by their own children in books and television shows. Internet crime buffs promoted suspects with websites, podcasts, and YouTube videos. Many opportunists exploited the tragedy to enjoy 15 seconds of fame, yet some people genuinely believed they had accomplished what no one else could and finally identified the Zodiac.

The usual suspects

William Joseph Grant was born in Winchester, Massachusetts on March 6, 1920. He enlisted in the U.S. Army in 1942 and was discharged in 1945. He also served as an Air Force radio operator in World War II. He later moved to Suisun, California and sold real estate in Fairfield. Grant was heavy-set, had a large face, wore glasses, and combed his dark hair in a pompadour.

In 1970, California Highway Patrol officer Lyndon Lafferty reported a strange encounter with Grant on a freeway. Lafferty was sitting in his parked patrol car when he noticed another vehicle nearby. The driver seemed to be watching the CHP officer. The two men engaged in what Lafferty described as "a cat and mouse game." After several incidents, Lafferty identified Grant as the driver and launched his own investigation.

Grant was reportedly trained in cryptography and became an instructor while he served in the army. Lafferty believed Grant was a man seen behaving erratically in a store at Moskowite Corner near Lake Berryessa on the day of the Zodiac attack. Vallejo police officer Steve Baldino identified Grant as a man who bothered Darlene at the restaurant where she worked and appeared in a suit at a painting party in her home. According to Lafferty, Darlene's sister, Linda, also identified Grant, although her sister, Pam, said he was not the sinister stranger who stalked Darlene before her death. Years later, Pam told a reporter from CBS 10 News in Sacramento that she was certain Grant was the stalker.

Vallejo police investigated Lafferty's claims and eventually dismissed Grant as a suspect. Handwriting analysis indicated Grant did not write the Zodiac letters and his fingerprints did not match suspected Zodiac fingerprints, including those found on the cab driven by the Zodiac's last-known victim, Paul Stine. Lafferty theorized Grant used the severed fingers of an unidentified victim to plant "fake" fingerprints on the cab. Lafferty also claimed that a judge had interfered in the investigation of Grant and protected the suspect for reasons unknown.

The 1986 book *Zodiac* included a chapter about Grant, but his name was changed to "Andrew Todd Walker." On February 2, 2012, Grant fell down at his home in Fairfield and he died from his injuries at the age of 91. On February 8, 2012, Lafferty released his book titled *The Zodiac Killer Cover-Up: The Silenced Badge*. He claimed Pam had betrayed his trust and somehow derailed the investigation of his suspect.

The projectionist

Joe Don Dickey was born in Slaton, Texas on March 13, 1926. He later used the name Richard Reed Marshall. In 1968, the *San Francisco Examiner* published two articles about Marshall and his love of nostalgia and old movies. In 1969, he lived in a basement apartment on Scott Street, several miles from the scene of the Zodiac's last-known murder in San Francisco. Marshall was employed at the KTIM radio station in San Rafael, California, before he went on to run the Port movie theater devoted to showing silent films. As a ham radio operator, Marshall made new friends and invited them to his home, but they were disturbed by the pornographic photographs of nude boys on display. These new friends were concerned and spoke to Marshall's former landlord. She complained that Marshall tried to take photos of her epileptic grandson who later died in what was described as a drowning accident. The friends came to believe that

Marshall was the Zodiac and contacted the Napa County Sheriff's Department. Investigator Ken Narlow explained that "certain oddities" about Marshall's background made him seem interesting on paper, but in reality he was not a very good suspect.

One witness recalled that Marshall once said he found something "much more exciting than sex." His favorite movie was the silent film titled *El Spectre Rojo*, or *The Red Phantom*, the name used in a possible Zodiac communication. Marshall's accusers claimed some Zodiac letters were reportedly written on teletype paper and their suspect owned a teletype machine. Marshall was ambidextrous and could write with both hands. He was heavy-set with dark hair and wore glasses.

Narlow asked a friend from the FBI to accompany him for an interview with the suspect. Marshall looked at photographs of the Zodiac victims but insisted he did not recognize any of the individuals. He then used his shirt sleeve to wipe away fingerprints on the photos. The interview lasted three hours, but Marshall denied any involvement in the Zodiac crimes. His fingerprints did not match any of the suspected Zodiac fingerprints. In 1986, Robert Graysmith's book, *Zodiac*, featured a chapter about Marshall, but his name was changed to Donald Jeff Andrews. Two decades later, the movie adaptation of Graysmith's book referred to Marshall as "Rick Martin."

In 1989, Marshall appeared in an episode of the television documentary series, *Crimes of the Century*, and said, "Obviously, if they had been more forthcoming, I would have understood why they were investigating me. My innocence notwithstanding, the details do fit." Richard Marshall died in a nursing home on September 8, 2008.

Man of many faces

Lawrence Klein was born on April 29, 1924, in the borough of Brooklyn in New York City. He served in the Navy and trained in electronics at the Navy's Radio Material School in Chicago, Illinois. Klein cared for his mother when she was afflicted with a severe illness, and the resulting stress led doctors to diagnose him as suffering from Psychoneurosis Hysteria. He was discharged from the Navy and moved to the Bay Area. In 1962, a car accident left Kane with partial brain damage and partial facial paralysis. His strange behavior soon generated a long record of arrests for burglary, prowling, and voyeurism. According to some accounts, Klein lived in an apartment at 217 Eddy Street, not far from the scene of the Zodiac's last murder. He often traveled to the Lake Tahoe area and moved to Las Vegas, Nevada in 1971. At some point, Klein began using the name "Larry Kane," along with other aliases.

Kane was first named as a Zodiac suspect by former Escalon police officer Harvey Hines. After a failed attempt to sue the department for age discrimination, Hines retired on a medical disability and developed an obsession with the Zodiac mystery. He believed the killer was responsible for the disappearance of nurse Donna Lass, and he was convinced she met Kane during her shifts at the Sahara Tahoe Hotel and Casino. Hines also believed Kane abducted and murdered 15-year-old Dana Lull in Las Vegas on April 27, 1974.

Years later, Hines wrote a lengthy report about the details of his investigation and his case against Kane. Hines believed the suspect matched the descriptions of the Zodiac. Kane was 5ft 9in tall with short, dark hair, had a "pot belly," and wore glasses. Hines speculated that Kane learned about cryptography in radio school. A Zodiac letter included the words "My name is---" and a cipher with 13 symbols.

Lawrence Klein aka Larry Kane.

Hines interpreted the symbols as a reference to Kane's date of birth and decoded the message to read, "name Kane." According to the report, Hines showed a photograph of Kane to Linda, a sister of Zodiac victim Darlene Ferrin. She tearfully identified the suspect as the man who stalked Darlene before she was killed. In 2002, Linda appeared at an event and said, "Do you want to know who the Zodiac is? It's Larry Kane!"

In 1994, Harvey Hines was featured in an episode of the tabloid television series *Hard Copy* with Kathleen Johns, a possible victim who claimed she was abducted by a man matching the description of the Zodiac in March 1970. Johns identified Larry Kane, but police had doubts about her ability to accurately identify the individual more than two decades after the incident. Survivor Michael Mageau identified suspect Arthur Leigh Allen in 1991, more than 20 years after the shooting at Blue Rock Springs Park in 1969. Allen did not match Mageau's description of the shooter. Mageau also stated that the killer had a face like another man depicted in the photo lineup of suspects. Investigators considered the identification unreliable and doubted Mageau's ability to accurately identify the shooter more than two decades later. In 2009, Vallejo police dispatcher, Nancy Slover, identified the voice of newspaper writer Richard Gaikowski as the man who called the police after the Blue Rock Springs attack. Slover's telephone conversation with the caller lasted less than one minute, and her identification raised questions about her ability to accurately identify the caller four decades later.

Vallejo police detective Ed Rust believed Larry Kane was a strong suspect, but Department of Justice agent Fred Shirasago stated there was no evidence linking Kane to the crimes. Vallejo police captain Roy Conway dismissed the Kane theory and claimed Kathleen Johns was shown a photograph of the suspect years earlier but failed to identify him. SFPD lieutenant Tom Bruton interviewed Kane and did not believe he was the Zodiac. In an interview for the Reelz channel documentary, *Zodiac: The Real Story*, Bruton said, "We had compared handwriting and fingerprints with what we had in the crime lab, and there was no matches there. The last big hope was the DNA comparison." Police obtained DNA from a suspected Zodiac communication, which did not match Kane's DNA profile.

Harvey Hines died on September 15, 2009, and Larry Kane died on May 20, 2010. More than ten years later, a French engineer named Faycal Ziraoui claimed he deciphered the Zodiac's "My name is--" code to reveal the letters, "KAYR," interpreted as a possible reference to Larry Kane. Ziraoui said his solution to the Zodiac's "Mt. Diablo code" included geographic coordinates that led to a location in South Lake Tahoe. In 2023, Ziraoui traveled to the United States and visited a remote site at West Lake Tahoe in California. Near the Hell Hole Reservoir, he examined a large formation of rocks which resembled a crossed-circle. Ziraoui was featured in articles published by *The New York Times* and *The San Francisco Chronicle*, and he appeared in the History Channel series, *History's Greatest Mysteries*.

Person of interest

Ross Mercer Stephen Sullivan was born on July 28, 1941, in Syracuse, New York, and the family moved to California. His mother died of cancer in 1959 and he lived with his father for some time. He enrolled at Riverside City College in 1961 and later became a library assistant. Ross struggled with mental health problems and his odd behavior led some members of the library staff to believe he might have killed Cheri Jo Bates in 1966. They noted that Ross usually wore the same clothes every day, but he changed his wardrobe after the murder. Ross was previously committed to the Patton State Mental Hospital in San Bernardino, California and he allegedly bragged that he had escaped.

In 1968, Ross lived in Santa Cruz, California, where he was arrested for indecent exposure. His mental health further deteriorated when his father died several months later. The Zodiac murders then began in December 1968. Jo Ann Bailey, Associate Professor of Library Services at RCC, sent a letter to *Vallejo Times-Herald* reporter Dave Peterson, with a list of reasons why Ross should be considered a suspect in the Bates case. Bailey said she contacted Riverside police but was informed that Ross had an alibi for the time Bates was killed.

Dave Peterson believed that some information indicated Ross may have been the Zodiac. He was interested in cryptography and methods to disguise handwriting. Ross appeared similar to the SFPD sketch of the Zodiac. He was 6ft 2in tall, weighed over 200 lbs, had blond hair in a crew cut, and wore dark-rimmed glasses. Peterson reported his theory to SFPD Inspector Dave Toschi and others, but police found no evidence linking Ross to the Bates murder or the Zodiac crimes. Ross Sullivan died in Santa Cruz on September 29, 1977.

The professor and the madman

Theodore John Kaczynski was born on May 22, 1942, in Chicago, Illinois. He was a quiet loner and a brilliant student. Ted skipped the sixth grade but had trouble adjusting to the social dynamics with older kids. Despite his emotional instability, he excelled in his studies of advanced mathematics and eventually graduated from Harvard University in 1962. Ted earned a master's degree and a doctoral degree in mathematics at the University of Michigan. By 1968, he lived in the San Francisco Bay Area and became the youngest assistant professor in the history of the University of California, Berkeley.

Ted's academic achievements were overshadowed by his erratic behavior and ongoing psychological problems. While at Harvard, Ted participated in a research experiment conducted by psychologist

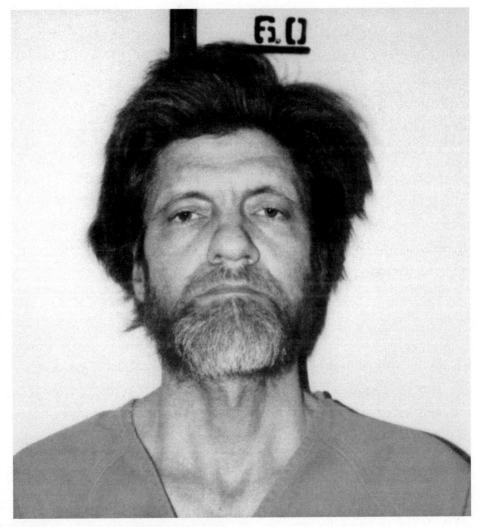

Ted Kaczynski aka "The Unabomber."

Henry A. Murray to study the effects of stress during interrogations. The test subjects were unaware of the true purpose of the experiment and were chosen in part because they were emotionally unstable. Ted and the other volunteers were instructed to write an essay about their philosophy of life. The subjects were told they would engage in a debate about their ideas but soon found themselves ridiculed in mock interrogations attacking their beliefs. The humiliating experience had lasting negative effects on Ted's mental state and sparked his intense hatred of psychologists. He became even more withdrawn and paranoid. In 1969, he suddenly resigned from his teaching position at UC Berkeley and then moved back to Illinois to live with his parents.

In 1971, Ted purchased a cabin in a remote area near Lincoln, Montana and began a new life alone in the woods. He survived with some financial help from his parents and occasionally made trips into a nearby town for supplies. Removed from society, Ted indulged his violent fantasies. He killed dogs and used a rifle to fire shots at passing airplanes in the sky. Ted was also enraged by any encroachment and sabotaged equipment at development sites in his area.

After years of isolation, Ted's hatred for modern technology and his desire to kill combined to create his criminal alter ego known as "The Unabomber," a name derived from his preferred targets, universities and airlines. Ted documented his thoughts and crimes in detailed journals, and wrote, "I often had fantasies of killing the kind of people I hated—i.e., government officials, police, computer scientists, the rowdy type of college students who left their beer cans in the arboretum, etc... My motive for doing what I am going to do is simply personal revenge. I do not expect to accomplish anything by it... I certainly don't claim to be an altruist or to be acting for the 'good' (whatever that is) of the human race. I act merely from a desire for revenge."

In 1978, Kaczynski mailed a package to an engineering professor at Northwestern University in Evanston, Illinois. A campus police officer suffered minor injuries when he opened the box and detonated the bomb inside. Almost one year later, another bomb injured a Northwestern student. Ted planted a bomb on an American Airlines plane at the O'Hare airport in Chicago, but the device malfunctioned and did not explode. The president of United Airlines was injured by a package bomb. Kaczynski sent more bombs to Brigham University in Utah, the Boeing airplane manufacturing company in Washington state, UC Berkeley, Yale University, and many other targets. Over a period of 17 years, Kaczynski injured 23 victims and killed three people.

Computer science professor David Gelernter was severely injured when a Unabomber package exploded at Yale University in 1994. Kaczynski sent the victim a letter which read, "People with advanced degrees aren't as smart as they think they are... If you'd had any brains you would have realized that there are a lot of people out there who resent bitterly the way techno-nerds like you are changing the world and you wouldn't have been dumb enough to open an unexpected package from an unknown source."

In 1995, the offices of the *New York Times*, the *Washington Post*, and *Penthouse* magazine received a letter from The Unabomber. The writer threatened to kill again unless a 35,000-word manuscript was published. Titled *"Industrial Society and Its Future,"* the essay condemned capitalism and blamed the industrial revolution for the destruction of the natural world. After the publication of the so-called "Unabomber Manifesto," Ted's brother, David, recognized the language and tone of the essay and he contacted the authorities.

FBI agents arrested Kaczynski and searched his cabin. More than 40,000 pages of handwritten journals were collected, including some encrypted in the bomber's secret code. Experts were unable to crack the code until Kaczynski's cipher "key" was discovered among his papers. FBI cryptographer Michael Birch was able to unlock the hidden text and reveal extensive entries about the Unabomber crimes. Kaczynski's own words provided a wealth of evidence for prosecutors to build a strong case. In 1998, he pleaded guilty to avoid the death penalty and was sent to a maximum-security prison in Colorado to serve a life sentence.

Theories linked the Unabomber to other crimes. At one time, investigators considered the possibility that Kaczynski was responsible for the 1982 "Tylenol murders" in the Chicago area. In 1996, *The San Francisco Chronicle* ran a story about two men who were convinced Ted Kaczynski was also the Zodiac. Douglas Oswell, a typesetter in Dover, Delaware, and California floor-covering estimator, Michael Rusconi, noted similarities between the Unabomber and Zodiac. Both killers used ciphers, sent taunting letters, and threatened to kill if their messages were not published. The Unabomber sent bombs and the Zodiac sent letters describing explosive devices. Kaczynski quit his teaching job shortly after the first Zodiac attack, he resembled the composite sketch of the Zodiac, and his handwriting appeared similar to the Zodiac's writing. Ted's background in mathematics could explain the Zodiac's reference to radians. Rusconi and Oswell presented their theory in a 1998 episode of the popular television series, *Unsolved Mysteries*. According to some accounts, handwriting comparisons indicated Kaczynski did not write the Zodiac letters and his fingerprints did not match suspected Zodiac prints. Kaczynski referred to Oswell as a "kook" and dismissed the claim that he was the Zodiac.

In 2021, Ted Kaczynski was diagnosed with late-stage cancer and transferred to a federal medical center in Butner, North Carolina. On June 10, 2023, the notorious Unabomber committed suicide by hanging himself in his cell.

Satan never sleeps

Bruce McGregor Davis was born in Monroe, Louisiana, on October 5, 1942, and grew up in Mobile, Alabama. After graduating from high school, Davis studied at the University of Tennessee before he moved to California in 1962. He drifted for some time and then returned to Tennessee to resume his education, but he was no longer interested in school and went back to California. In 1965, he started using marijuana, speed, LSD, and other psychedelic drugs. According to Davis, his life changed forever in 1967 when he decided to accompany a friend who was returning a borrowed saw to a "crazy" man and a group of drug-addled girls at a house in Topanga Canyon. The man was Charles Manson, an ex-convict with a long criminal record for charges including burglary, petty larceny, auto theft, armed robbery, check forgery, and procuring prostitution as a pimp. After serving a ten-year sentence in a federal prison on McNeal Island in Washington state, Manson was released in 1967 and traveled to California where he soon attracted a small group of loyal followers who were impressed by his charisma and religious preachings.

Manson called his group "the family" and he often used drugs and psychological manipulation to indoctrinate the members of his impressionable flock. He claimed to be the messiah Jesus Christ and promised to lead his people to safety in a coming race war between whites and blacks. Manson referred to the impending apocalypse as "Helter Skelter," named after a song by the legendary rock band The Beatles. Debate continues regarding his true motives, but Manson eventually convinced "the family" to murder innocent human beings to help launch the race war and fulfill his prophecy.

On the night of August 9, 1969, family members, Tex Watson, Susan Atkins, and Patricia Krenwinkel, entered the property at 10050 Cielo Drive, located in the hills of Benedict Canyon on the west side of Los Angeles. Watson shot and killed a young man named Steven Parent, who was visiting the caretaker in a guest house. Coffee heiress Abigail Folger, writer Wojciech Frykowski, and Hollywood hair stylist Jay Sebring were inside the main house with their friend, actress Sharon Tate, the wife of director Roman Polanski, known for his controversial occult horror film, *Rosemary's Baby*. The invaders surprised Tate and her guests, and Watson declared, "I'm the devil, and I'm here to do the devil's business." Krenwinkel, Watson, and Atkins then stabbed and shot the victims. They tried to hang Sharon Tate and stabbed her 16 times.

At the time, another Manson associate named Bobby Beausoleil was in jail on charges for killing music teacher Gary Hinman. Beausoleil stabbed Hinman and used his blood to write the words "political piggy" on a wall. According to Susan Atkins, Manson told his followers to "leave a sign, something witchy," at the Tate crime scene in order to convince investigators that Beausoleil was innocent and that the real killers were still on the loose. Atkins used Sharon Tate's blood to write the word "pig" on the front door of the house.

On August 11, Manson directed his killers to a house on Waverly Drive in Los Angeles. Watson, Atkins, and Krenwinkel were accompanied by Leslie Van Houten and Linda Kasabian. Businessman Leno LaBianca and his wife, Rosemary, were stabbed dozens of times. Krenwinkel used the blood of the victims to write the words "Rise" and "Death to pigs" on a wall, and she scrawled the phrase "Healter Skelter" on a refrigerator door.

Manson and the others were later arrested for the Tate/LaBianca murders, and Bruce Davis was charged for his participation in the killings of Gary Hinman and ranch hand Shorty Shea. Davis confessed and was convicted on counts of robbery, conspiracy to commit murder, and first-degree murder. He was sentenced to life in prison and remained loyal to Manson until he converted to Christianity and became a preacher.

Shortly after the Tate/LaBianca murders, some observers noted that the Zodiac also left a handwritten message at a crime scene, and speculation soon led to theories about possible connections between the two cases. California Department of Justice special agent Mel Nicolai and SFPD inspector William Armstrong investigated members of the Manson family and found no evidence of any link to the Zodiac crimes. In his book *The Family*, writer Ed Sanders reported that Inyo County district attorney Frank Fowles believed the Zodiac and Manson cases were connected, but he could not provide any evidence to support his theory. In his 1987 book *Manson: Behind the Scenes*, former secret service agent Bill Nelson wrote that a "well respected, reliable source" told him that the Los Angeles District Attorney's Office orchestrated a massive conspiracy to conceal the truth behind the Manson murders. Nelson's source claimed the cover-up was conceived in a secret meeting after items used in the Zodiac crimes were discovered during the Manson investigation.

The source of the conspiracy story was Howard Davis, author

of a 1997 book published by Nelson titled *The Zodiac/Manson Connection*. Davis cited a "pristine source" inside the LA D.A.'s office with direct knowledge of the cover-up who claimed that the hood worn by the Zodiac was found during a search of items belonging to Bruce Davis. According to this version of events, officials consulted "a legal expert" and decided to hide the evidence because they feared a Zodiac prosecution could somehow undo the previous convictions for the Hinman and Shea murders and set Bruce Davis free. The authorities in Southern California chose not to prosecute Bruce Davis because they wanted to avoid the high cost of a multi-million-dollar trial. Howard Davis also claimed the source said the investigators decided to orchestrate the conspiracy to obstruct justice because their wives and girlfriends had grown weary of the long work hours in the Manson case. The conspiracy tale relied on several implausible premises. Bruce Davis confessed his involvement in the Hinman and Shea murders, and a Zodiac prosecution would have no effect on those cases or his convictions. Authorities in Southern California would not bear the financial burden of a Zodiac prosecution in Northern California. Competent and responsible investigators would not conceal evidence linking the Manson and Zodiac crimes because their wives and girlfriends were tired of the heavy workload.

Howard Davis eventually identified his "pristine source" in the D.A.'s office as his ex-brother-in-law, a former federal prosecutor who briefly worked as an investigator for the Manson prosecution. Davis claimed the brother-in-law told him about the conspiracy during a conversation in 1974. Years later, the brother-in-law denied making such statements to anyone and referred to Howard Davis as "a nutjob" who had "no credibility." Davis also claimed that his Manson/Zodiac theory was endorsed by Vincent Bugliosi, the man who prosecuted Charles Manson and co-wrote the book, *Helter Skelter*. According to Davis, Bugliosi was initially skeptical about the theory but later changed his mind after seeing compelling evidence. In reality, Bugliosi dismissed the idea that Manson was somehow behind the Zodiac murders. "I've never heard of anything to support that allegation," Bugliosi said. "I doubt it very much. I think it would have come out by now." After learning that Davis said he had endorsed the Zodiac/Manson theory, Bugliosi denied the claims and rejected the entire conspiracy story as "preposterous on its face and obviously 100 percent wrong." Bugliosi asked, "If Manson committed more murders than the Manson murders, why would anyone want to protect him on that? It makes no sense. What you're talking about is a crime, obstruction of justice... a massive conspiracy of many, many people being involved, for no believable reason... It would serve no end that would help the perpetrators (of the conspiracy)... I just find the allegation absolutely inconceivable... I reject it completely out of hand."

Bruce Davis was often named as a Zodiac suspect and the conspiracy story was repeated as fact despite the lack of evidence. Manson/Zodiac theories were absorbed into other revisionist accounts linking Manson to satanic cults, the "Son of Sam" killings in New York, and many infamous crimes. In San Quentin State Prison, Davis largely ignored questions about the Zodiac case and had no incentive to confess his involvement in other murders while he petitioned for early release. Davis was deemed eligible for parole seven times between 2010 and 2021, but California governors consistently refused to release him back into society. In 2022, a board denied his request for parole and said Davis still lacked empathy for the victims.

Daddy did it

In 1999, Dennis Kaufman watched the Learning Channel television documentary *Case: Reopened* and noticed that the infamous sketch of the Zodiac killer resembled his estranged stepfather, Jack Tarrance. Kaufman quickly developed theories linking Tarrance to virtually every aspect of the Zodiac crimes. He was featured in several news segments with CBS reporter Cris Pickel in Sacramento, California and launched a website to promote his suspect. Kaufman announced he had discovered a roll of film, which purportedly showed dead bodies of unidentified victims, but the images did not support his claims. Kaufman also declared that he found a black Zodiac-like hood in an amplifier owned by his stepfather. The hood did not match the description of the killer's costume provided by surviving victim, Bryan Hartnell.

Kaufman joined forces with a woman who advertised her services as a handwriting expert, and she soon concluded that Tarrance was the author of the Zodiac letters. Eventually, Kaufman's theory expanded and named Tarrance as the Chicago Lipstick Killer, the Black Dahlia killer, the Texarkana Phantom, the Cleveland Torso killer, and even the author of the ransom note in the murder of six-year-old beauty pageant contestant JonBenét Ramsey. Kaufman self-published a book, *The Man Behind the Mask*, and was featured in the television show *True Crime with Aphrodite Jones* in 2010. Dennis Kaufman died in 2018, but another theorist continued his legacy in the book called *The World According to Jack Tarrance: The Real Zodiac Killer, Black Dahlia Avenger, Get Hoffa Squad Member, and More.*

Bizarre confessions

Guy Ward Hendrickson was born on March 3, 1915, in Velva, McHenry, North Dakota. He worked as a carpenter, married, and fathered six children, including two daughters, Janice and Deborah. Hendrickson died in Los Angeles on October 24, 1983, at the age of 68. On April 29, 2009, Deborah Perez and her disbarred attorney Kevin McLean held a press conference in front of the *San Francisco Chronicle* offices to announce her deceased father as the Zodiac. Deborah said Hendrickson confessed on his deathbed that he had done "bad things," and she later recovered long-dormant memories of his killing spree. McLean told reporters that Deborah was examined by psychologists, but he conceded that skeptics would question her credibility.

Deborah's story was shocking and included her own confession that she had assisted her father during the Zodiac crimes. She claimed that she had written some of the Zodiac letters and placed stamps on the envelopes. Deborah said she accompanied Hendrickson on the night of the Zodiac's last-known murder of cab driver Paul Stine. She also claimed that she had sewn together the hooded costume worn by the Zodiac at Lake Berryessa.

Deborah displayed a pair of dark-rimmed glasses she claimed belonged to Paul Stine. San Francisco police investigated her claims and concluded the glasses did not belong to the victim. Deborah's sister, Janice, rejected the Zodiac accusations and said she did not believe her father was a murderer. After news reports about Deborah's press conference, true crime writer, M. William Phelps, revealed that he had worked with Perez to examine her story but abandoned the project when she claimed to be the illegitimate daughter of assassinated president John F. Kennedy.

Sins of the father

George Hill Hodel Jr. was born in Los Angeles on October 10, 1907. He was an intelligent child who scored 186 in an IQ test and graduated from high school when he was 15 years old. Hodel attended the California Institute of Technology in Pasadena, graduated from Berkeley, and then completed his medical education at the University of California in San Francisco. He later earned a degree in psychiatry, remained in Hawaii for some time, then moved to the Philippines and lived overseas until 1990. In the course of his life, Hodel married and divorced four women and fathered several children. George Hodel died in San Francisco at the age of 91 on May 17, 1999.

In 2006, retired police detective Steve Hodel published a book titled *Black Dahlia Avenger: The True Story*. Hodel claimed his deceased father was responsible for the murder of 22-year-old Elizabeth Short, also known as "The Black Dahlia." On January 12, 1947, Short's nude body was found on a vacant lot on South Norton Avenue in a residential neighborhood of Los Angeles. The victim had been cut in half above the waist using the surgical technique referred to as a hemicorporectomy. The killer sliced the corners of her mouth open to her ears in what has been dubbed "the Glasgow smile." Some of Short's flesh had been cut away and the killer also slashed at her breasts and thigh. The body was drained of blood at another location before the victim was dumped in the vacant lot.

Twelve days after Short's body was discovered, an envelope arrived at the offices of the *Los Angeles Examiner* newspaper. The sender used cut-and-paste letters to create the words, "Here is Dahlia's belongings, letter to follow." Short's birth certificate, photographs, business cards, and an address book were included with the message. A handwritten letter read, "Here it is. Turning in Wed., Jan. 29, 10 am. Had my fun at police. Black Dahlia Avenger." The writer stated that he would surrender at a specific location but never showed up. Another letter read, "Have changed my mind. You would not give me a square deal. Dahlia killing was justified."

The Black Dahlia case was never solved and the story became one of the most infamous mysteries in true crime history. Theories linked Short's murder to Hollywood elites, secretive sex cults, and other sinister groups. Many men were investigated as possible suspects, including George Hodel. The doctor apparently referred to the victim in telephone conversations recorded by police. "Supposin' I did kill the Black Dahlia. They can't prove it now. They can't talk to my secretary anymore because she's dead. They thought there was something fishy. Anyway, now they may have figured it out. Killed her. Maybe I did kill my secretary." Hodel was named in a grand jury report, but the evidence was insufficient to prosecute. Years later, Steve Hodel claimed he found photographs of Short among his father's possessions, but her family said the woman was not Elizabeth. Steve hired a handwriting expert, who concluded that Hodel had written some of the letters attributed to the Dahlia killer. Hodel's daughter claimed he had raped and impregnated her, but he was acquitted in a trial. Steve Hodel was convinced his father used bribery to avoid punishment for the crime. According to Steve, George Hodel held powerful secrets and officials allowed him to escape justice because his arrest for the Dahlia murder would expose police corruption, implicate prominent figures, and destroy careers at the highest levels. Steve referred to this conspiracy as "Dahliagate."

In 2009, Steve Hodel published a second book, *Most Evil: Avenger, Zodiac, and the Further Serial Murders of Dr. George Hill Hodel.* Steve now believed his father was also many other notorious villains,

including the Zodiac, the Chicago "Lipstick killer," the Los Angeles "Werewolf," and the "Jigsaw" killer in Manila. Steve Hodel's efforts to link his father to the Zodiac crimes relied heavily on speculation, assumptions, and theories about the geographic locations and geometric relationships of the crime scenes. *Most Evil* included many geographic and geometric errors and Hodel's placement of the crime scenes were often inaccurate. Hodel's expert-for-hire concluded that George Hodel had written the Zodiac letters.

In 2015, Steve Hodel published a third book, *Most Evil II: Presenting the Follow-Up Investigation and Decryption of the 1970 Zodiac Cipher in which the San Francisco Serial Killer Reveals his True Identity.* In 2018, Hodel published a fourth book titled *Black Dahlia Avenger III: Murder as a Fine Art: Presenting the Further Evidence Linking Dr. George Hill Hodel to the Black Dahlia and Other Lone Woman Murders.* Hodel believed he was presenting a strong and compelling case that his father was a ruthless and prolific serial killer, but critics noted the lack of any solid evidence to support his theories.

George Hodel was 62 years old at the time of the Zodiac's last-known murder in 1969. The oldest estimate of the suspect's age ranged somewhere between 35 and 45 years old. Hodel did not resemble the composite sketch of the Zodiac and he did not match the eyewitness descriptions of the killer. Hodel had a mustache for most of his life, but witnesses described the Zodiac as clean shaven. Steve Hodel speculated that his father traveled to the United States to commit the Zodiac crimes, but produced no solid evidence that placed the suspect in the relevant areas on the dates of the attacks.

Steve Hodel appeared in television episodes of *20/20*, the *Today* show, and *HLN's Very Scary People*. In 2023, he published a work of "historical fiction," *Black Dahlia Avenger IV*. George Hodel's granddaughter wrote a memoir titled *One Day She'll Darken: The Mysterious Beginnings of Fauna Hodel*. The book inspired the TNT television mini-series, *I Am the Night*, starring actress India Eisley.

Son of the Zodiac

Earl Van Best Jr. was born in Wilmore, Kentucky on July 14, 1934. He spent his early years in California and Japan. After graduating from high school, Best attended San Francisco City College. His first marriage ended in divorce and he worked as a book salesman. In 1961, the 27-year-old Best was outside Herbert's Sherbet Shoppe in San Francisco when he met a 13-year-old girl named Judy Chandler. He became obsessed with Judy and took her to Reno, Nevada, where they were married. The marriage was annulled one month later. A grand jury indicted Best on charges of conspiracy, child stealing, and statutory rape. While out on a $5,000 bail bond, Best fled with Judy and they traveled through several different cities to avoid capture. In December 1962, they stopped in New Orleans, and Judy gave birth to a baby boy named Earl Van Dorne Best on February 12, 1963. Best was not interested in the responsibilities of fatherhood and he abandoned the child at an apartment building in Baton Rouge. Best was arrested in April and Judy returned to her family. The baby was adopted by a loving family and renamed Gary Loyd Stewart. Earl Van Best Jr. died in Mexico on May 20, 1984. Judy later married Rotea Gilford, the first black inspector in the San Francisco Police Department.

Decades after he was adopted, Gary Stewart contacted Judy and established a relationship with his birth mother. He wanted to learn about his biological father and was disturbed by the truth

about Earl Van Best's dark past. In 2004, Stewart was watching a television documentary about the Zodiac case when he noticed his father resembled the composite sketch of the elusive killer. Stewart was soon convinced Earl Van Best Jr. was the Zodiac.

Ten years later, HarperCollins published a book written by Gary Stewart and Susan Mustafa, *The Most Dangerous Animal of All: Searching For My Father and Finding the Zodiac Killer.* Stewart recounted his family background and offered speculation to connect his father to the Zodiac crimes. According to Stewart, Earl Van Best Jr. was associated with Anton LaVey's Church of Satan and knew Bobby Beausoleil, a biker linked to the Manson family. Best was reportedly a fan of Gilbert and Sullivan, the creators of *The Mikado* musical quoted by the Zodiac. Stewart claimed his biological father served a sentence at the Atascadero hospital for the criminally insane. Mustafa and Stewart believed their solutions to the Zodiac ciphers revealed Best's name. The authors noted that a line visible in an image of a suspected Zodiac fingerprint corresponded to a scar on Best's right index finger. The book also presented examples of handwriting attributed to Best, including his marriage certificate and related papers. Documents examiner Michael Wakshull concluded that Best had written the Zodiac letters.

In a CNN interview with Erin Burnett, Stewart said, "I believe for the first time in the history of this case that I have presented more evidence than has ever been presented on any one suspect." In reality, the case against Earl Van Best Jr. quickly fell apart under scrutiny. Days after the publication of Stewart's book, Zodiac theorist Mike Rodelli contacted the church where Best was married and inquired about the handwriting on the marriage documents. The reverend of the church was apparently responsible for the writing, a fact that rendered Wakshull's conclusion invalid. When informed that he based his opinion on writing that did not belong to Best, Wakshull speculated that the reverend was Best's accomplice.

The proposed fingerprint match relied on the baseless assumption that the image of the suspected Zodiac fingerprint had been somehow reversed as a mirror image. This reversal was necessary to align the possible scar in the suspected Zodiac fingerprint on the correct side with the scar on the Best fingerprint. Zodiac cipher expert David Oranchak demonstrated that the cipher solutions revealing Best's name were of little value since the same methods produced many other names in the Zodiac ciphers.

Gary Stewart claimed San Francisco police compared his father's DNA to suspected Zodiac DNA but could not eliminate him as a suspect. Stewart also said he consulted with experts who told him that his familial DNA was similar to the Zodiac DNA. The experts did not have access to the Zodiac DNA, but Stewart produced his own Zodiac profile using information he obtained from an image in a television show about the case. The image in question was actually a mock facsimile of a DNA profile created specifically for the show. Stewart based his DNA claims on a fictional DNA profile that never existed.

The SFPD refused to cooperate with Stewart and Susan Mustafa described the reason as the "hook" of their book. Stewart's birthmother Judy married SFPD inspector Rotea Gilford, a close friend of San Francisco Mayor Willie Brown and former Mayor Dianne Feinstein. In 1971, Gilford joined the homicide detail and was later involved in the investigation of the so-called "Zebra murders" by a group of radical black muslims, who targeted white victims in order to ignite a race war. Gilford became a prominent figure in the police department and

Bay Area politics. Stewart and Mustafa suggested that the SFPD was embarrassed by Gilford's relationship with the ex-wife of the Zodiac and therefore refused to cooperate with the authors as they exposed the most notorious serial killer in American history.

In March 2020, the FX network aired a four-part documentary titled *The Most Dangerous Animal of All*. The mini-series initially focused on Stewart's family drama and then dismantled his theory in the final episode. A fingerprint expert rejected the claim that Earl Van Best's fingerprint somehow matched a suspected Zodiac fingerprint. The show also presented the facts debunking the proposed handwriting and DNA matches. The producers obtained a copy of Best's criminal record and discovered there was no evidence he was ever incarcerated at the Atascadero prison hospital for the criminally insane. During her on-camera interview, Susan Mustafa said Gary Stewart transcribed Best's criminal record in their research for the book and apparently added the Atascadero entry. Mustafa resented the betrayal and referred to Stewart as a "motherfucker." She declared her intention to burn the book they wrote together but continued to appear with her co-author in media interviews. At the end of the series, Gary Stewart dismissed the facts which disproved his claims and sped off in his BMW with a vanity license plate that read, "Van Best."

The series also included a final revelation, which apparently eliminated Earl Van Best Jr. as a Zodiac suspect. One of Best's other children wrote a letter stating that he was in Austria at the time of the Zodiac crimes and did not return to the United States until 1971. If this timing of events was accurate, Best could not have been the Zodiac.

New arrivals

Gray Francis Poste was born in Potsdam, St. Lawrence, New York on November 8, 1937, and later moved to Lyons Falls, New York. He joined the U.S. Air Force and was assigned to the Rockville radar station. On the morning of January 9, 1959, Poste suffered severe injuries to his brain and skull in a car accident in which another airman died. He recovered, but his forehead was permanently scarred. Poste was transferred to another radar station in Greenland and later moved to California. He married, fathered a son, and worked for decades as a house painter. In 2016, Poste was arrested on felony charges of domestic violence after he allegedly pushed his wife down a flight of stairs. A court ruled he was mentally incompetent to stand trial and Poste was committed to a state hospital. He died in Stockton on August 23, 2018.

In 2021, a group issued a press release identifying Gary Francis Poste as a suspect in the Zodiac murders. The "Case Breakers" consisted of more than 40 members with law enforcement, military, forensic, academic, legal, and investigative skill sets. The group was led by a writer named Thomas J. Colbert, co-author of a book about the still-unsolved case of the airline hijacker "D.B. Cooper," titled *The Last Master Outlaw: How He Outfoxed the FBI Six Times—but Not a Cold Case Team*. Colbert also produced the History channel documentary, *D.B. Cooper: Case Closed*. The press release stated Poste was implicated by an escape map, photos, dual identities, cryptic clues, and shell casings. Some people who knew Poste claimed he confessed, was obsessed with killing, tortured and killed animals, loved to antagonize police, and built bombs similar to the explosive devices described in Zodiac letters. The informants also said Poste owned many weapons and buried his arsenal in the woods.

The Case Breakers tried to link their suspect to the 1966 murder of Riverside City College student Cheri Jo Bates and noted Poste was reportedly undergoing a medical exam at the March Air Force base located approximately 15 miles from the scene of the crime. Riverside police were not impressed by the evidence presented by the Case Breakers and publicly rejected theories connecting the Zodiac to the Bates murder.

Poste's accusers argued that he matched the description of the Zodiac and scars on his forehead were similar to scars on the forehead of the killer as depicted in a police sketch. The Case Breakers press release featured a photograph of Poste with a circle around his forehead and the SFPD sketch of the Zodiac with lines on the circled forehead. The lines were nothing more than wrinkles added to the drawing as artistic flourishes, and none of the witnesses ever described the Zodiac with forehead scars.

According to the Case Breakers, the Zodiac writings included hidden messages found only by using Poste's name as a key, and the deciphered clues would be revealed in a book by retired Georgia television news anchor, Dale Julin.

Paul Alfred Doerr Jr. was born in Sharon, Pennsylvania, on April 1, 1927. He joined the Navy in 1945 and was discharged in 1946. Doerr married a woman named Rose, who gave birth to their daughter Gloria. In the early 1960s, the family moved to Solano County in the San Francisco Bay Area. Doerr had many interests and hobbies, and he was later known for publishing "zines" on a variety of subjects, including self-sufficient living and science fiction. Paul Doerr died of a heart attack on August 2, 2007.

In 2022, writer Jarett Kobek published a book about the Zodiac case, *Motor Spirit: The Long Hunt for the Zodiac*. His second book,

How to Find Zodiac, named Paul Doerr as a suspect and presented a collection of facts to connect him to the crimes and letters. Kobek and his theory were featured in many media outlets, including *Los Angeles Weekly.* Paul Haynes, co-author of a book about the Golden State Killer, was convinced Kobek had finally identified the Zodiac and declared the chances that Doerr was the killer were higher than with any other person on earth. Haynes and others believed Kobek's book contained compelling evidence.

The Zodiac placed several one-cent stamps on an envelope sent to San Francisco attorney, Melvin Belli. The stamps were difficult to process, and Paul Doerr once sent a letter to a newspaper encouraging readers to use one-cent stamps to harass the postal service. Both Doerr and the Zodiac spelled the word "cipher" as "cypher" and drew arrows with feathers on the ends. Doerr used a variation of a crossed-circle symbol in one of his writings. Doerr's daughter said he listened to the same recording of the Gilbert and Sullivan musical *The Mikado* quoted by the Zodiac. Doerr reportedly owned weapons and was shown in a photograph with a knife sheath on his belt. In a "letter to the editor," Doerr made statements that some people interpreted as a cryptic murder confession. According to one account, Doerr claimed he attended a party at a large estate where wealthy guests hunted human beings like wild animals. Doerr and the Zodiac both wrote bomb formulas using ingredients such as fertilizer and ammonium nitrate.

The case against Doerr seemed similar to the lists of bullet points compiled to accuse many other suspects, and some of the entries were less compelling upon closer examination. Most homemade bombs contained similar ingredients, including fertilizer and ammonium nitrate, and these formulas were not unique to Doerr or the Zodiac.

Claims that Doerr confessed to murder relied on the assumption that his vague statements referred to killing, while other interpretations could justify different conclusions. Doerr may have listened to the *Mikado* recording and used similar language as the Zodiac, but he was not the only suspect matching those characteristics. The Zodiac did place one-cent stamps on an envelope, but the majority of his communications were sent with other stamps. Like Doerr and the Zodiac, millions of Americans also used one-cent stamps.

Jarett Kobek believed Paul Doerr was a viable suspect, but conceded he could be wrong. He hoped police would investigate and confirm his suspicions or eliminate Doerr. Kobek wrote a 19-page report detailing the evidence against Doerr and sent the information to the San Francisco Police Department. Doerr might have looked like a good suspect on paper, but investigators knew that long lists of seemingly compelling points often amounted to nothing more than interesting trivia. The SFPD never responded to Kobek's report.

Amateur sleuths added many other names to the long list of men identified as the Zodiac, and each new theory offered a variation of the same elements linking a suspect to the crimes. Police frequently received tips from people who believed they had solved the case, but the killer's motives and true identity remained a mystery.

CHAPTER 6:
INSPIRATIONS

"You can always count on a murderer for a fancy prose style."
Vladimir Nabokov

The Zodiac was unique, a serial killer who wore a bizarre costume, sent taunting letters, and offered cryptic clues as to his identity. Yet some elements of the Zodiac's crimes and writings indicated he might have been inspired by other criminals and popular culture.

Murder by design

In 1921, the weekly crime and mystery magazine *Detective Story* published a short story by Edwin Baird titled "Z." The villain kills bank presidents and sends messages in red envelopes. The killer calls a local newspaper and says, "This is Z calling. I've just killed Reeves of the Second National." Z is finally identified as a deranged investor who killed the banker "leeches" as revenge for his financial losses.

On the night of June 11, 1930, 39-year-old grocer Joseph Mozynski and his 19-year-old mistress, Catherine May, were sitting in a car parked in a secluded spot in the New York borough of Queens when a man wearing a dark hat and coat appeared with a gun. He shot Joseph in the head and then searched through Catherine's purse. The man burned some of Catherine's personal letters and later escorted her to a trolley stop. He spoke with a heavy German accent as he gave

Catherine a piece of paper and told her not to read the message until the next day. The note read, "3X3-X-097."

A local newspaper received a letter on June 13. "Kindly print this letter in your paper for Mozynski's friends: CC-NY ADCM-Y16a DQR-PA . . . 241 PM6 Queens. By doing this you may save their lives. We do not want any more shooting unless we have to." The letter was signed "3X." Another letter accurately described the ammunition and weapon used by the killer. The writer referred to Mozynski as a "dirty rat" who had taken important documents and warned that 14 of Joseph's friends would be killed unless the documents were recovered.

The killer returned on June 16th and targeted another young couple sitting in a car parked in the Queens neighborhood of Creedmore. The gunman demanded the male victim's driver's license and then said, "You're the one we want. You're going to get what Joe got." The man shot the victim twice in the head and then searched his pockets. Police later found an article about the previous murder in the victim's pocket with the words "here's how" written in pencil. The killer gave another note to the female victim.

Another letter arrived with two spent shell casings. Other messages were sent to the *New York Evening Journal* newspaper and the New York Police Department. All of the communications were signed with the same 3X signature and an inverted letter "V." Joseph Mozynski's brother, John, also received a threatening letter in Pennsylvania. One letter offered an unbelievable explanation for the killings. The writer claimed he was a member of an international secret organization of spies known as the Red Diamond of Russia and the victims were former members who had stolen important material. The letter read, "The last document, N.J. 4-3-44 returned to us the 19 at 9 PM. My mission is ended. There is no further cause for worry." The murders and letters stopped, and the case was never solved.

The body of 20-year-old Alfred "Bud" Lord was discovered on a dock along the Mississippi river in New Orleans, Louisiana on November 11, 1931. He had been shot once in the head and the gun was found in the water. Days before his death, Lord claimed that a man was trying to kill him, but police believed he had invented the story and staged his suicide to look like a murder. A handwritten note was pinned to Lord's overcoat which read, "He accidentally knew too much. Too bad!" A crossed-circle was drawn below the text.

In Richard Connell's 1924 short story, *"The Most Dangerous Game,"* hunter Sanger Rainsford is trapped on a remote island and hunted by a murderous Russian aristocrat known as Count Zaroff. After years of killing wild game, Zaroff discovers the thrill of hunting human beings for sport. The 1932 film adaptation became a classic that inspired many other films such as *A Game of Death*, *Open Season*, and *Surviving the Game*, and episodes of the television shows *Gilligan's Island*, *Criminal Minds*, *The Simpsons*, and more.

The 1939 film, *Charlie Chan at Treasure Island*, featured a villain named Dr. Zodiac, who sends taunting letters to *The San Francisco Chronicle*. The legendary detective Chan describes the killer as a criminal egoist who enjoys laughing at police and suffers from a disease known as "pseudologia fantastica." This condition is characterized by the habitual or compulsive tendency to lie in stories intended to impress others and portray the liar as important. Dr. Zodiac is exposed as the blackmailing mystic Fred Rhadini, played by actor Cesar Romero.

Legendary western movie actor, Tim Holt, was featured as the cowboy hero Red Mask in a long-running comic book series from 1938 to 1955. In the June-July issue published in 1952, a character named Lady Doom captures Red Mask and plans to kill him by a method selected from the options on her spinning "Death Wheel," including water, fire, rope, gun, and knife. In 1970, *San Francisco Chronicle* reporter Paul Avery received a suspected Zodiac message with the phrases "by fire, by gun, by knife, by rope."

Echoes in the darkness

Zodiac letters referred to an "electric gun sight" used to target victims in darkness. "What I did was tape a small pencel flash light to the barrel of my gun. If you notice, in the center of the beam of light if you aim it at a wall or celling you will see a black or darck spot in the center of the circle of light about 3 to 6 inches across. When taped to a gun barrel, the bullet will strike exactly in the center of the black dot in the light." A similar idea was mentioned in a 1961 episode of the television series *Alfred Hitchcock Presents*, "Museum Piece." A hunter named Ben uses a rifle with a light attached to the barrel, as narration provided by his father explains, "He'd invented a fool proof gadget for night shooting. A spotlight mounted on his .22 in such a way that his shot would strike the exact center of light." Ben accidentally shoots a young man and is sent to prison, but then someone murders the district attorney and the killer remains at large. Ben's father says, "I remember the excitement of the manhunt. The most dangerous game."

On January 11, 1967, the ABC network broadcast an episode of the cult classic TV show *Batman*, titled "The Zodiac Crimes." The Joker and The Penguin (actors Cesar Romero and Burgess Meredith) join forces in a series of kidnappings and robberies based on the 12 signs of the astrological Zodiac. A letter from The Joker reads, "I've come to announce a new crime wave for Gotham City. This is the first of the zodiac crimes. Look for 11 more, and don't forget to keep score." The Zodiac was also mentioned in an episode about another villain named "The Puzzler," titled "The Duo is Slumming." In 1964, issue #323 of the Batman title *Detective Comics* included another bad guy named "The Zodiac Master," who predicts the future and wears a costume with the 12 signs of the Zodiac. Batman, Robin, and Superman team up against the evil "Doctor Zodiac" in a 1966 issue of the comic book *World's Finest*.

Actor Raymond Burr was famous for his starring role in the hit television show *Perry Mason* (1957–1966) and he returned to the crime genre in the late-1960s for the NBC series, *Ironside*. Burr portrayed Robert T. Ironside, a San Francisco police chief paralyzed by a sniper's bullet. In the episode "Perfect Crime," broadcast on March 7, 1968, Ironside lectures in a criminology class at Bay College. When a student asks about the concept of the perfect crime, Ironside warns that no crime is perfect and criminals will be caught. An anonymous note challenges Ironside and says, "Dear Chief Ironside, you are wrong. The perfect crime is possible. I will prove it."

After class is dismissed, a gunman watches Ironside and others through a rifle scope and then shoots a student. The editors of the *San Francisco Dispatch* and another Bay Area newspaper receive identical typed letters apparently sent by the shooter. Ironside believes the gunman is a brilliant, cold, and calculating man who satisfies his enormous ego by writing letters to the newspapers for attention. The sniper tracks Ironside to his home and opens fire, wounding officer Eve Whitfield. Ballistics tests prove a different weapon was used in the two shootings. Ironside reminds officers and viewers that different weapons do not automatically indicate two shooters. A suspect on the college rifle team named Jonathan Dix is shot but survives, so the shadow of suspicion falls on another member of the team, Larry Wilson. Ironside makes himself a target by setting a trap and the sniper shoots a dummy in a wheelchair. Dix is then caught just as he is about to stage Wilson's suicide to mislead investigators. Ironside concludes Dix staged his own shooting and framed Wilson for the sniper attacks.

Several details of the *Ironside* episode were similar to elements of the Zodiac crimes, including a gunman using a .22 caliber weapon and sending identical letters to the editors of Bay Area newspapers. In the episode, a crossed-circle is superimposed over the potential victims as they are viewed through a rifle scope. The killer used a .22 caliber gun to murder the victims in the first Zodiac attack on Lake Herman Road, but a 9-millimeter gun was used in the second shooting at Blue Rock Springs Park. The Zodiac mailed identical letters to the editors of Bay Area newspapers and signed his messages with the crossed-circle symbol. "Perfect Crime" aired nine months before the murders on Lake Herman Road, and the first Zodiac letters were sent in July 1969. The Zodiac may have imitated aspects of the television episode.

From Hell

A suspected "Zodiac" letter sent to the *Los Angeles Times* in 1971 referred to police as "Blue Meannies," a term first introduced in the 1968 animated classic *Yellow Submarine*, featuring songs by The Beatles. The movie includes characters known as Blue Meanies, blue human-like creatures who hate colors and music. Blue Meanies became a popular slang term used to describe police in Britain. In 1970, Alameda County sheriff's officers dressed in blue outfits responded to riots at the California People's Park in Berkeley and were nicknamed Blue Meanies by protestors. The term was also used to describe police in the movie, *Vanishing Point*, released on March 13, 1971. The Zodiac letter which mentioned "Blue Meannies" was postmarked on the same date.

The letter sent to the *Los Angeles Times* newspaper stated, "I do have to give them credit for stumbling across my riverside activity, but they are only finding the easy ones, there are a hell of a lot more down there." The writer seemed to suggest that the Zodiac was responsible for the unsolved 1966 murder of Riverside City College student Cheri Jo Bates. Riverside police first speculated about the possible Zodiac connection in 1969 and *Chronicle* reporter Paul Avery presented the theory to the public in November 1970, four months before the *LA Times* letter appeared to confirm the Zodiac link to the Riverside murder. Skeptics believed the Zodiac did not kill Bates but took advantage of the publicity attributing the murder to him and played along to pad his criminal resume and misdirect the investigation. Someone mailed three virtually identical handwritten letters in the Riverside case, and the Zodiac mailed three virtually identical, handwritten letters. The "Confession" letter sent to a Riverside newspaper and local police stated, "SHE SQUIRMED AND SHOOK AS I CHOAKED HER, AND HER LIPS TWICHED." In one letter, the Zodiac wrote that he would torture his victims "over ant hills and watch them scream + twich and squirm." The similar language and the misspelling "twich" could indicate the Zodiac may have imitated the text of the confession letter after reading about the case. A January 1969 issue of *Inside Detective* magazine featured a

six-page story about the Bates murder along with a reproduction of the Confession letter.

Some of the writings in the Riverside and Zodiac cases were reminiscent of letters attributed to the most infamous serial killer in history, Jack the Ripper. Many investigators and experts believed the Ripper letters were actually written by attention-seeking hoaxers or ambitious newspaper reporters who exploited the frenzy of publicity surrounding the murders. Pranksters and real killers who sent taunting letters often imitated the style and tone of the Ripper letters, including spelling errors, mocking authorities, bold threats of future violence, and a macabre sense of humor. The Ripper letters, the Riverside "Confession," and the Zodiac messages shared common elements, including a writer portraying himself as a powerful killer of superior intelligence. One Ripper message read, "The next job I do I shall clip the ladys ears off and send to the police officers just for jolly wouldn't you." The Riverside Confession letter read, "I lay awake nights thinking about my next victim... I shall cut off her female parts and deposit them for the whole city to see." A Zodiac letter stated, "I shall (on top of everything else) torture all 13 of my slaves that I have wateing for me in Paradice... Others shall have pine splinters driven under their nails & then burned. Others shall be placed in cages & fed salt beef untill they are gorged then I shall listen to their pleass for water and I shall laugh at them." Another Ripper letter was accompanied by a human kidney. Three Zodiac letters were sent with bloodstained pieces of a victim's shirt.

The devil you know

Like the Ripper mystery, the Zodiac story was rewritten and influenced popular culture as the killer was transformed into an archetypal villain in fiction, film, and television. In the 1979 episode of the TV series *Lou Grant* titled "Samaritan," the *Los Angeles Tribune* newspaper receives what appears to be a letter from a serial killer after five years of silence. The Samaritan claimed credit for the murders of several hitchhikers and stranded motorists. Each letter quoted the Bible from The Book of Luke, Chapter 10, and the story of the "good samaritan" who helped those in need. The new Samaritan letter reads, "I am back with you for sure," and ridicules Bill Birgin, the lead detective assigned to the original investigation, "Say hello to that pig Birgin for me." Crime reporter Jim McCrea is obsessed with Samaritan, but could not sell his book about the case and complains, "Publishers like books with endings, and Samaritan didn't have an ending." McCrea is thrilled when he lands a publishing deal thanks to Samaritan's return, but Birgin dismisses the new letters as forgeries because the writer quotes from a different version of the Bible than the original messages from the killer. City editor Lou Grant finally exposes McCrea as the forger and the reporter confesses that he missed the excitement of the Samaritan mystery. The story dramatized elements of the 1978 scandal surrounding accusations that SFPD Inspector David Toschi had forged some Zodiac letters.

Toschi served as the inspiration for the character of SFPD detective Jon Lucca in the 1996 movie *The Limbic Region*. Actor Edward James Olmos (*Miami Vice*, *Battlestar Galactica*) stars as the alcoholic burnout haunted by his failure to catch "The Scorekeeper," a serial killer who murdered couples in lovers lanes and sent taunting letters in the mid-1970s. Diagnosed with a terminal illness and driven to solve the case, Lucca confronts his prime suspect, Lloyd Warden, portrayed by George Dzundza (*The Deer Hunter*, *Law & Order*). The two men are soon locked in a psychological battle, which ends in a

violent showdown. Warden's character was loosely based on Zodiac suspect, Arthur Leigh Allen.

Author William Peter Blatty was disturbed by the 1974 Zodiac letter that referred to the film adaptation of his book, *The Exorcist*, as a satirical comedy. In Blatty's sequel, *Legion*, a detective is baffled by the inexplicable return of the executed "Gemini Killer," who mailed taunting letters and carved the astrological sign of Gemini on his victims. Serial killer Jeffrey Dahmer developed an obsession with Blatty's 1990 film, *The Exorcist III*, and even showed the movie to one of his victims.

In a 1996 episode of the TV series *Nash Bridges* titled "Zodiac," a cab driver is shot and killed at the location of the Zodiac's last-known murder, the intersection of Washington and Cherry Streets. The killer sends a letter which begins, "This is the Zodiac speaking. I'm back." SFPD Inspector Nash Bridges (actor Don Johnson) teams up with the lead detective of the original Zodiac task force and they quickly conclude the killer is a copycat. A cipher and other clues lead to a diner and the investigators arrive just in time to prevent the Zodiac imposter from killing a waitress. Bridges then answers a telephone call from a man who says, "Just wanted to congratulate you on catching the copycat Zodiac killer. Maybe someday you might even catch me."

A Zodiac-like villain resurfaces after years of silence in a 1998 episode of the TV series *Millennium* titled "The Mikado." Former FBI profiler Frank Black (actor Lance Henriksen) pursues "Avatar," an infamous serial killer responsible for several murders years earlier. Avatar sends taunting letters and coded messages as he kills his victims in live-streamed videos posted on the internet. Black interprets the clues and tracks Avatar to a trailer rigged with bombs.

The trailer explodes and a body is found in the debris, but Black is convinced Avatar somehow managed to escape justice and is still at large.

The TV series *Criminal Minds* rehashed the Zodiac story in the 2012 episode titled "True Genius." A young couple sitting in a parked car in a secluded spot are killed by a gunman wearing a hood with a crossed-circle on his chest. The killer leaves a large crossed-circle on the windshield of the victim's car. Police also find what appears to be a piece of a shirt worn by the Zodiac's last-known victim, cab driver Paul Stine. The killer stabs a young couple by a lake and then shoots a cab driver. Agents of the FBI's Behavioral Analysis Unit discover a genius chess player is re-enacting the crimes to impress a childhood friend who shared a fascination with the Zodiac mystery. As teenagers, the two friends killed a little boy just for fun. The episode combined elements of the Zodiac story and the case of teenagers Nathan Leopold Jr. and Richard Loeb, who murdered a 14-year-old boy because they wanted to experience a thrill.

Deliver us from evil

The 2005 film, *The Zodiac,* presented a fictional account of the Zodiac case and focused on Matt Parish, a Vallejo police detective obsessed by the hunt for the killer. Director Ulli Lommel's 2005 low budget movie, *Zodiac Killer,* followed a copycat in Los Angeles killing victims who neglect or abuse the elderly. In Lommel's sequel, *Curse of the Zodiac,* a writer receives messages from the real Zodiac and tries to help a psychic stripper who sees visions of the murders.

Life imitated art and art imitated life in the 2007 film, *Zodiac.* In one scene, SFPD Inspector David Toschi (actor Mark Ruffalo) sits in a movie theater and watches *Dirty Harry.* The movie was inspired

by the Zodiac and the title character was reportedly inspired by Toschi. *Zodiac* also included a brief cameo by surviving victim Bryan Hartnell.

The television series *Riverdale* featured a mysterious serial killer known as Black Hood, who targets victims he believes to be sinners. The character was first introduced as a superhero in issue #9 of *Top-Notch Comics*, published in October 1940 by MLJ Comics (which later became Archie Comics). Black Hood was a former police officer wrongfully convicted for a crime he did not commit. He becomes a vigilante delivering justice to evil-doers. Black Hood was featured in a 1944 radio serial and various comic book titles until 1947. He reappeared in Red Circle Comics in 1983, Impact/DC Comics in 1991, and Dark Circle Comics in 2015. In the *Riverdale* TV series, Black Hood shoots couples in lovers lane locations and sends taunting letters and coded messages.

Author Meg Gardiner's crime thriller, *Unsub*, featured a Zodiac-inspired villain known as "The Prophet," who returns to the San Francisco Bay Area after two decades of silence and resumes his campaign of terror with more murders, taunting messages, and cryptic clues. The killer marks the bodies of his victims with the ancient symbol for Mercury, messenger of the gods and guide to the underworld. Detective Mack Hendrix led the original investigation and suffered a nervous breakdown. Twenty years later, The Prophet targets Mack's daughter, FBI profiler Caitlin Hendrix.

Screenwriter Matt Reeves said the Zodiac inspired the reimagined version of the comic book villain, The Riddler, in the 2022 film *The Batman*. Accountant Edward Nashton invents The Riddler persona and terrorizes the people of Gotham City with a series of elaborate attacks against prominent figures he deems guilty of corruption. He sends greeting cards and ciphers and also wears a costume with a symbol similar to the Zodiac's crossed-circle. The Batman studies the clues and tries to solve the puzzles as The Riddler plants bombs and commands his deranged followers to kill helpless citizens.

Several copycat killers and imposters were inspired by the Zodiac, including the "Zodiac" church arsonist in New York, the "Son of Zodiac" in New York, the Kobe school killer in Japan, and Edgar Patino in North Carolina. Other notorious criminals imitated some of the Zodiac's methods. David Berkowitz, aka "The Son of Sam," and Wichita's "B.T.K. Strangler," Dennis Rader, wrote taunting letters, and Rader even called police to report one of his murders. In the 1990s, truck driver Keith Jesperson murdered eight women, sent taunting letters, and left a handwritten confession on a wall in a public restroom. Jesperson signed his messages with a happy face and became known as "The Happy Face Killer."

In 2021, someone sent strange letters to television stations, religious institutions, businesses, and government agencies in Connecticut, New Hampshire, Pennsylvania, Vermont, New Jersey, New York, and Washington D.C. One message was delivered to the White House. The writer threatened to kill a bus driver and claimed he murdered several victims and ate their flesh. "EVERY MONTH SINCE NOVEMBER I HAVE KILLED BOTH MALE AND FEMALES. IT IS POSSIBLE THAT I AM KILLING INDIVIDUALS WHOSE IDENTITIES ARE IMPOSSIBLE TO TRACK (I.E., HOMELESS, RUNAWAYS, ILLEGAL IMMIGRANTS), AND DESTROYING ALL EVIDENCE SO EFFICIENTLY." Some of the messages were signed with the name of British author and occultist Aleister Crowley, while others were signed "The Chinese Zodiac Killer." Investigators from the New York State police, the U.S. Postal Inspection Service, and the FBI's Joint Terrorism Task Force tracked the letters and set up surveillance at post offices. In May 2022, Jesse Bartlett, a resident of LaFargeville, New York, was arrested after he dropped 42 brown envelopes at collection boxes in Clayton and Watertown. The 45-year-old bus driver confessed that he had written "Zodiac" letters, but police found no evidence to indicate he had ever killed or eaten anyone. Bartlett pleaded guilty and was sentenced to serve 16 months in prison. The hoax proved the ghost of the Zodiac still haunted the world almost fifty years after he vanished without a trace.

CHAPTER 7:
ENDINGS

"Evil is unspectacular and always human,
and shares our bed and eats at our own table."
W. H. Auden

The Zodiac case remained unsolved while other infamous villains were finally captured. Gary Ridgway, aka "The Green River Killer," murdered dozens of women in Washington state during the 1980s and 1990s, and he was identified by DNA evidence in 2001. Dennis Rader, aka "The B.T.K. Strangler," killed men, women, and children from 1974 to 1991, and he confessed in 2005 when confronted with DNA evidence linking him to the crimes. Joseph James DeAngelo was known as "The Golden State Killer," "The East Area Rapist," "The Visalia Ransacker," and "The Original Night Stalker." He was responsible for 120 burglaries, 51 sexual assaults, and 13 murders in California between 1974 and 1986. DNA and genetic genealogy identified DeAngelo in 2018 and he pleaded guilty to avoid the death penalty. The arrest raised hopes that modern technology could also solve the Zodiac mystery.

Over the years, the search for evidence that could identify the Zodiac left investigators frustrated, and the public was often confused by answers many people did not expect and few wanted to hear after decades of dead ends.

Fingerprints were found on the cab driven by the Zodiac's last-known victim and San Francisco police believed some belonged to the killer. SFPD lieutenant Tom Bruton submitted the fingerprints to the FBI's Automated Fingerprint Identification System (AFIS). The computer scanned and compared millions of fingerprints and produced a match. A set of prints on the rear bumper of the cab identified a man who had a job washing cabs in 1969. He was African-American and did not match the description of the killer, so police eliminated him as a suspect.

In 2001, the SFPD crime lab lifted a palm print from the "Exorcist" letter. Police could not retrieve the evidence in 1974 because the sender had written over the print. Modern techniques separated the print, which was then used for comparison with suspects. In an interview for the television show, *Cold Case Files*, Susan Morten of the crime lab stated that the print did not match the palm prints of the left and right hands of the prime suspect, Arthur Leigh Allen.

Lessons in chemistry

San Francisco police submitted some of the Zodiac messages for DNA analysis in the late-1990s. Some of the Zodiac envelopes were examined, including those sent with the October 1969 letter claiming responsibility for the murder of cab driver Paul Stine, the November 9 letter complaining about police lies, and the message sent to attorney Melvin Belli. These three letters each contained a piece of Stine's bloodstained shirt. Other tested items included the envelopes sent with the "dripping pen" card accompanied by the Z340 cipher, the "My Name is" cipher, the Dragon card, and the "Mt. Diablo code." Few cells were recovered from those communications. A letter referring to the failed abduction of possible Zodiac victim Kathleen Johns was sent on July 24, 1970. Two days later, a five-page letter quoted at length from the Gilbert and Sullivan musical, *The Mikado*. A letter describing the horror movie *The Exorcist* as a satirical comedy was sent in January 1974. The envelopes mailed with those communications were processed for DNA and cells were found. A DNA sample was obtained from the 1978 Zodiac forgery, which mentioned Inspector Dave Toschi. Tom Voigt posted a SFPD crime lab document regarding the DNA testing on his website zodiackiller.com.

In interviews, retired SFPD inspector Vince Repetto and Lt. Tom Bruton said DNA was obtained from a suspected Zodiac communication and the profile did not match the DNA of suspects Arthur Leigh Allen and Larry Kane. SFPD inspectors Mike Maloney and Kelly Carroll requested another round of DNA testing in 2001. Dr. Cyndi Holt conducted the tests in the SFPD DNA lab and examined several suspected Zodiac envelopes and letters. A strand of hair found behind a stamp seemed to confirm eyewitness descriptions of a man with reddish-brown hair. Dr. Holt appeared in the ABC documentary series *PrimeTime* and said a partial DNA profile of a male was obtained from a stamp on the envelope that contained the "dripping pen" card and the Z340 cipher. Dr. Holt explained that the partial profile was not sufficient to positively identify an individual but might be used to "narrow suspicions" or "eliminate suspects." The profile did not match Allen and other suspects included in the DNA comparisons.

Critics argued the DNA profile was contaminated and compromised because the samples were taken from the front and back of stamps, and any DNA obtained from those samples could belong to individuals who handled the envelope, such as postal workers, newspaper staff, or even police. Mike Rodelli accused a suspect who was eliminated by the DNA profile, and he questioned the results in his book titled *In the Shadow of Mt. Diablo: The Shocking True Identity of the Zodiac Killer.* Rodelli stated that *S.F. Chronicle* reporter Kevin Fagan said the DNA profile was actually a mixture of genetic material obtained from different areas of the suspected Zodiac communications and the samples were combined to create sufficient material necessary for the testing. In one online posting, Rodelli suggested authorities knew the DNA profile was useless and staged the DNA presentation for the *PrimeTime* show to scare the Zodiac and create the illusion that police had evidence that could identify him.

Alan Keel served as the director of the SFPD DNA lab during the late-1990s, and he stated that most of the suspected Zodiac communications did not contain genetic material sufficient for DNA comparison. Keel speculated that the lack of genetic material indicated the sender did not lick the stamps. The theory could explain the absence of any usable DNA under the stamps or flaps of the envelopes sent with Zodiac letters.

Saliva and oral epithelial cells were found on two messages. According to Keel, DNA from the 1978 forgery matched DNA from a 1974 letter. The SFPD concluded the 1978 letter was not authentic and Keel's story of a DNA match meant at least one of the suspected Zodiac messages sent in 1974 was also considered a forgery.

In 2017, Vallejo police detective Terry Poyser requested DNA testing of two Zodiac envelopes. He was optimistic and believed the crime lab would present results within weeks. Years passed without any confirmed reports about Vallejo police efforts to find DNA evidence. Meanwhile, the Napa County Sheriff's Office submitted a bottle found at the Berryessa crime scene, a bloodstained blanket, and pieces of plastic clothesline to the Department of Justice DNA lab in Richmond, California. Testing reportedly produced a mixture of DNA with a partial genetic profile that could not be isolated from the other DNA sources. The mixture most likely included the blood of the two victims stabbed at Lake Berryessa. Gloves found in the cab driven by Zodiac victim Paul Stine were also examined. Pam Hofsass, Director of the Forensic Services Division for Contra Costa County, said blood on the outside of the gloves belonged to Stine and DNA found inside the gloves belonged to an unidentified male.

The confusion continued in May 2024 when Mike Morford, podcaster and founder of Zodiackillersite.com, stated that authorities had developed four full DNA profiles from Zodiac "letters and evidence." He cited two unnamed sources but he was unable to provide any further details to explain which law enforcement agencies were involved, from which items the DNA had been obtained, or if the sources were referring to DNA evidence mentioned in previous media reports. According to Morford, both of his sources confirmed that none of the profiles matched each other. After he posted the news online, Morford said that one of the sources revised the information and stated one or more of the profiles were only partial profiles. A partial profile might be used to exclude suspects but that DNA would not be sufficient to identify any individuals using genetic genealogy. Absent specific details, the news was met with a combination of skepticism and cautious optimism by those who hoped DNA could someday identify the Zodiac. Speculation produced various explanations for the seemingly problematic evidence, including theories that some of the DNA belonged to postal workers, employees at the San Francisco Chronicle newspaper, members of law enforcement, and others who handled the suspected Zodiac communications. DNA found on the outside of an envelope or on the front of a stamp could possibly be attributed to someone who touched those items. DNA found under a stamp or envelope flap most likely belonged to the person or persons who sent the letters unless they convinced an unwitting accomplice or a co-conspirator to lick the stamps and envelope flaps for them. Multiple DNA profiles belonging to different people could indicate more than one person was responsible for the letters but investigators had to identify those individuals in order to determine their connection to the Zodiac communications. The presence of DNA belonging to several people could be explained if they all knew the same suspect and licked stamps for him. Those people may have been unaware of the crimes but the true extent of their involvement may never be known if they are no longer alive and cannot be questioned. The minimal information revealed by the unnamed sources could seem to support a variety of scenarios as news of possible Zodiac DNA evidence once again provided few answers and raised many more questions.

Victims of circumstance

DNA did not identify the Zodiac, but genetic evidence did solve other mysteries. In 1986, a Placer County sheriff's deputy discovered a human skull along Highway 20 and Interstate 80, near Emigrant Gap and west of Donner Pass in California's Sierra Nevada mountains. The skull was taken to the coroner's office, but the cause of death could not be determined and the identity of the person remained unknown. In 2023, police in South Lake Tahoe sent the skull to the California Department of Justice Bureau of Forensic Services for analysis. DNA taken from the skull was compared to DNA obtained from the family of Donna Lass, the nurse who disappeared from the Tahoe area in 1970. A suspected Zodiac postcard sent in March 1971 with the phrase "pass Lake Tahoe areas" was interpreted as a reference to Lass and she was often cited as a possible Zodiac victim. Investigators and amateur sleuths had searched for Lass's body and developed theories about the location of her remains. The skull was found approximately 70 miles northwest of where Lass was last seen in Stateline, Nevada.

In January 2024, the Placer County Sheriff's Office and South Lake Tahoe police announced that DNA from the skull matched DNA from the Lass family. The cause of death and the location of Donna's body were still unknown. News headlines exploited the Zodiac connection, but SLTPD detective Sgt. Nick Carlquist said the investigation did not uncover any evidence that the Zodiac abducted or killed Donna Lass.

New revelations cast doubts on theories linking the Zodiac to another possible victim. In August 2021, the Riverside Police Department released a statement regarding writings associated with the 1966 murder of Cheri Jo Bates. Six months after the crime, someone mailed three letters to Riverside police, the *Riverside Press-Enterprise* newspaper, and the victim's father Joseph Bates. Written in block form with a pencil, the message read, "Bates had to die. There will be more." Two of the notes were signed with a small symbol resembling the letter Z. California Department of Justice documents examiner Sherwood Morrill concluded the three letters were written by the same person who produced the Zodiac letters, but other experts disagreed. Riverside police were the first to propose the Zodiac as a suspect in the Bates murder, but the department later reversed its position and rejected claims of a Zodiac connection. RPD instead focused on a man who allegedly knew the victim, even though DNA taken from hairs found in Cheri Jo's hand did not match the suspect. Some observers believed the lack of a DNA match seemed to support speculation that the Zodiac killed Bates, but the RPD declared an end to the popular theory that the killer wrote the letters.

The press release stated: "In April 2016, investigators received an anonymous letter postmarked from San Bernardino, California. This letter was typed and appeared to have been generated from a computer. The author of the anonymous letter admitted to writing the handwritten letters. The author apologized for sending the letters and said it was a sick joke. The author admitted that he was not the Zodiac killer or the killer of Cheri Jo Bates and was just looking for attention. In 2020, the Homicide Cold Case Unit and the FBI Los Angeles Investigative Genealogy Team submitted the stamp from the letter for additional DNA analysis and subsequent interviews were conducted. The individual linked to the DNA evidence on the stamp admitted to writing the letter and sending it to Riverside Police Department. The author was a young teenager at the time and had a troubled youth. He said he wrote the letter seeking attention and was remorseful for his actions. Investigators confirmed, the person was not involved in the murder of Cheri Jo Bates or involved in the murders associated with the 'Zodiac Killer.'"

The bombshell news was followed by a curious statement. "Additional information was developed regarding a separate set of letters sent to Northern California police agencies. The author claimed to be the 'Zodiac Killer,' but the author ultimately admitted to sending the letters to keep the investigation going." The RPD release seemed to state that the man who confessed he had written the "Bates had to die" letters also confessed that he had written Zodiac letters

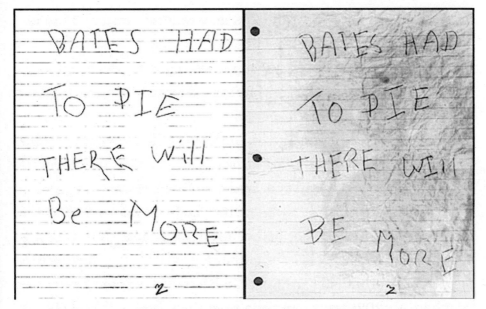

According to Riverside police, these letters were "a sick joke" by a hoaxer.

sent to "Northern California police agencies." None of the suspected Zodiac letters were mailed to law enforcement agencies in Northern California. A Zodiac letter was sent to the office of San Francisco attorney, Melvin Belli, but the majority of the Zodiac messages were sent to Bay Area newspapers and *The Los Angeles Times*. The RPD either referred to previously unknown Zodiac letters or mistakenly stated that Zodiac letters were sent to police agencies. The press release did not specify which Zodiac letters were written by the hoaxer and did not explain how police confirmed he was the author of those communications. The vague language of the press release left open the possibility that one person wrote the "Bates had to die" letters and a second person was responsible for the Zodiac writings sent to agencies in Northern California.

Riverside police had exposed another impostor and created more confusion about the origins and authenticity of the Zodiac letters.

Sherwood Morrill believed the Zodiac wrote the "Bates had to die" letters, but his conclusion would be invalid if based on writings now attributed to the hoaxer. Opinions of other experts who believed the Zodiac letters were written by one person would be questioned if a hoaxer sent some of those messages.

The RPD release did not mention the "Confession" letter mailed by someone who claimed to be the killer. Unlike the other Riverside writings, the letter was typed, but the envelope was addressed in distorted block printing. Some of the language in the Confession was similar to the Zodiac, including the misspellings of the word "twiched." Riverside police initially believed the killer had written the Confession but later dismissed the letter as a hoax. The Zodiac may have written the Confession or simply imitated the tone and content in his own messages. Riverside police did not state the person who wrote the "Bates" letters was also the author of the Confession, indicating their theories required yet another hoaxer.

The Devil's arithmetic

The final chapter in the story of one Zodiac imposter was revealed when computer technology and human ingenuity solved a baffling mystery. In November 1969, the Zodiac sent a greeting card with a cipher containing 340 symbols. Many people proposed solutions using various methods, but no one had deciphered the hidden text. Expert cryptographers and amateur codebreakers were captivated by the challenge of the Z340 cipher and some compared notes and shared information on internet forums. Three men in three different countries across the globe met online and hoped their combined knowledge of computer programming and cryptography could crack the Zodiac's cipher.

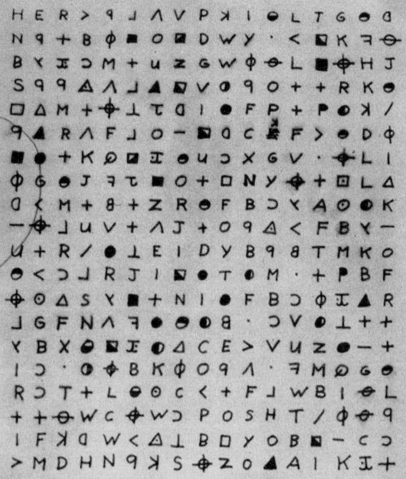

The Z340 cipher.

Software developer and cryptologist David Oranchak had been working on challenging problems for more than 25 years. He earned a Master of Science degree in Computer Science from National Technical University/Walden and a Bachelor's degree in Computer Engineering from Virginia Tech. Oranchak worked in many areas of industry and levels of government, including the Defense Intelligence Agency, the Department of Justice, and the codebreaking unit of the FBI. In 2007, publicity surrounding the release of the movie *Zodiac* led him to a website where he saw the 340 cipher and was instantly fascinated by the cryptic clue. "I have a computer programming background and a fondness for puzzles," Oranchak said, "so I was naturally drawn to the idea of using computers to help me solve the problem. I began running experiments and collecting information about the ciphers, which culminated in developing the zodiackillerciphers.com website as a place to organize it all."

In 2013, Oranchak collaborated with Jarl Van Eycke, a computer programmer in Flanders, Belgium. "Jarl followed a similar path as me. He has programming experience and became interested in the Zodiac ciphers, and wanted to write software to explore his ideas about ways of possibly solving Z340. He joined the forums around 2013 and exchanged information with me and several others who were also working on the ciphers from a scientific point of view." Van Eycke developed AZdecrypt, software Oranchak described as a "fast and powerful cipher solver." Van Eycke and entrepreneur Louie Helm used a modified version of the software to set a world record for deciphering of a bigram substitution of the shortest cipher length.

In 2019, Oranchak received a message from Sam Blake, who earned a PhD in mathematics at Monash University in Melbourne, Australia. "Being a mathematician, he had some really intriguing ideas about how to chip away at the space of possible transcription schemes," Oranchak said. "We eventually started working on experiments together. He developed many thousands of transposition variations to try out with the hopes that one of them might happen upon the correct scheme." Blake explained his role in the process. "My main contribution here was actually enumerating many possible reading directions through the cipher, in total over 650,000. David and I both ran these through azdecrypt and zkdecrypto respectively."

The trio soon found a small yet important piece of the puzzle. "It was a needle in a haystack," Blake recalled. "Even finding the right haystack to search in was lucky." Oranchak was surprised when fragments of a message seemed to appear. "We saw a glimmer of the real plaintext in one of the 650,000+ transposition variations Sam produced. I noticed some Zodiac-like phrases in one of the results. So we all really focused on that one until we unravelled the entire message by figuring out exactly how the transposition scheme worked." The partial solution was not correct but did suggest information about the cipher's construction. Oranchak realized the Z340 was not like the Zodiac's first cipher, a relatively simple substitution cipher reading from left to right. "By luck, we discovered that (Zodiac) split it into three pieces and rearranged the message in a predictable diagonal pattern in the first two pieces."

The Z340 thwarted previous attempts to crack the code, and the resemblance to the Z408 led many people to falsely assume the two ciphers were similar and could be solved with the same methods. Oranchak explained the complex construction of the Z340. "It is a transposition cipher mixed with homophonic substitution, and split into 3 sections. Solving it requires identifying the three sections, the transposition schemes, and some errors in the 2nd section. The first two sections (9 lines each) use a 'right 2, down 1' reading rule to unravel the plaintext once the substitution key has been applied. The last two lines contain words where some are in the normal reading direction and some are reversed. How he actually put the cipher together is speculative: Maybe he applied the reading rule directly to fill the grids. Or, maybe he used a simple triangular scheme."

The Zodiac's first cipher was solved in a few days by Donald and Bettye Harden, and the killer may have been disappointed when that part of his game ended so quickly. He might have intended to make his second cipher more difficult to solve and carefully arranged the elements of the Z340 to confound codebreakers. "He definitely reacted to the Hardens solution and made it much harder," Oranchak said. "Cracking it required undoing those arrangements then trying to discover his substitution key. That wasn't enough because he made some mistakes in the second piece. Jarl discovered the mistakes and corrected them, which greatly cleared up the second piece." The decryption was adjusted to include Van Eycke's corrections, and the solution began to materialize.

While deciphering the first nine lines of the message, Oranchak realized their strategy worked. "I fed some of those phrases above into AZdecrypt as 'cribs' to solve the first section. AZdecrypt produced the entire plaintext for the first section, which included 'THAT WASN'T ME ON THE TV SHOW'. Upon seeing that phrase I knew for certain it was a real message from Zodiac, since it referred to the Jim Dunbar show incident that happened two weeks prior to him sending the 340." On October 22, 1969, the Zodiac imposter known as "Sam" spoke with Melvin Belli during the broadcast of the popular television talk show hosted by Jim Dunbar. Sam claimed to be the Zodiac and the sensational episode made national news. The reference to the Dunbar show was a strong indication that the real Zodiac watched or heard about the incident and felt compelled to defend his reputation in the hidden text of the Z340 cipher. "It was an amazing moment," Oranchak said. "I shared the result with Sam and Jarl and they were both equally stunned and excited that we had finally gotten onto the right track. We worked together to uncover the rest of the message. We had a nugget of a solution on Thursday. I took Friday off and worked on it all day. My teammates Sam and Jarl also worked on it a lot."

Van Eycke resolved the remaining issues with the decryption by Saturday morning and then Oranchak submitted a report to the FBI codebreakers. The Bureau soon responded with an informal confirmation of the solution. "When I talked to the FBI, they only needed to make one change to the solution." The team had deciphered a section of six letters to read, 'soo her.' "We couldn't figure out the part that says, 'soo her,' [but] their cryptanalyst called me and she said she thinks it's supposed to say 'sooner' instead." The FBI delayed a public statement about the solution so agents could notify the families of the victims.

Crack proof

On December 11, 2020, Oranchak posted the solution on his website and the news spread across social media. The FBI issued a press release which read: "The FBI has a team of cryptanalysis experts that decipher coded messages, symbols, and records from criminals known as the Cryptanalysis and Racketeering Records Unit. CRRU regularly works with the cryptologic research community to solve ciphers. On December 5, 2020, the FBI received the solution to a cipher popularly known as Z340 from a cryptologic researcher and independently verified the decryption. Cipher Z340 is one of four ciphers attributed to the Zodiac Killer. This cipher was first submitted to the FBI Laboratory on November 13, 1969, but not successfully decrypted. Over the past 51 years CRRU has reviewed numerous proposed solutions from the public—none of which had merit. The cipher was recently solved by a team of three private citizens. The Zodiac Killer case remains an ongoing investigation for the FBI San Francisco division and our local law enforcement partners. The Zodiac Killer terrorized multiple communities across Northern California and even though decades have gone by, we continue to seek justice for the victims of these brutal crimes. Due to the ongoing nature of the investigation, and out of respect for the victims and their families, we will not be providing further comment at this time."

The solution was also confirmed by other cryptographers, and German computer scientist, Joachim von zur Gathen, published a paper titled "Unicity distance of the Zodiac-340 cipher," with further analysis demonstrating the solution was correct. Within hours of the announcement that the cipher had been solved, the story circulated worldwide and news reports named Dave Oranchak, Jarl Van Eycke, and Sam Blake as the men who finally solved one of the most baffling mysteries in the Zodiac case. "This could have only happened with the two other guys I worked with," Oranchak said. "No way I could have done any of this without them." Van Eycke was proud of their teamwork. "It is unbelievable how everything came together so perfectly between the three of us, and I am so happy to be a part of it."

Investigators, reporters, researchers, crime buffs, and many others who had studied the Zodiac letters recognized the familiar tone and voice of the Zodiac in the deciphered solution. Like the message hidden in the Z408, the text of the Z340 repeated the killer's fantasies about possessing his victims in the afterlife.

I HOPE YOU ARE HAVING LOTS OF FUN IN TRYING TO CATCH ME THAT WASN'T ME ON THE TV SHOW WHICH BRINGS UP A POINT ABOUT ME I AM NOT AFRAID OF THE GAS CHAMBER BECAUSE IT WILL SEND ME TO PARADICE ALL THE SOONER BECAUSE I NOW HAVE ENOUGH SLAVES TO WORK FOR ME WHERE EVERYONE ELSE HAS NOTHING WHEN THEY REACH PARADICE SO THEY ARE AFRAID OF DEATH I AM NOT AFRAID BECAUSE I KNOW THAT MY NEW LIFE IS DEATH LIFE WILL BE AN EASY ONE IN PARADICE

The Z340 cipher was sent along with a handwritten note that read, "I though you would ncad a good laugh before you hear the bad news you won't get the news for a while yet." The "bad news" may have been the revelation that the Zodiac was not the person who called the television station or a reference to the next letter with the Zodiac's warning that he would no longer announce his crimes. The phrase could also be interpreted as a vague hint regarding some unknown future victim or the Zodiac's plan to murder children with bombs.

During the Jim Dunbar television show in October 1969, the Zodiac imposter known as "Sam" said he was afraid that he would be hurt and attorney Melvin Belli promised to help the killer avoid the gas chamber. The Z340 solution clearly stated that Sam was not the Zodiac and claimed the real killer was not afraid of execution. The Zodiac apparently believed his cipher would be solved, but he most likely never expected the solution would only come five decades later when no one would be surprised by his denial.

Many people were disappointed that the cipher solution did not include the killer's name, a reference to previously unknown victims, or some other clue that could help solve the case. Theorists who had developed elaborate theories about the Z340 rejected the solution, while others adapted to the new information. Oranchak acknowledged that some people might be confused by the solution. "It may be hard to convey to the general public because it does require additional steps— diagonal reading, splitting into three seconds, fixing the mistakes, and rearranging letters in the last two lines."

Cryptographers acknowledged Oranchak, Van Eycke, and Blake for their historic achievement. "We gave keynotes at the HistoCrypt and American Cryptogram Association conferences," Oranchak said. "I also co-presented the solution with the FBI at the American Academy of Forensic Sciences conference." Oranchak appeared in several television documentaries and produced a YouTube video series titled *Let's Crack Zodiac*. He appreciated messages from young people who said the story of the Z340 solution inspired them to learn more about cryptography.

Some amateur codebreakers wondered if the same methods could crack the Zodiac's unsolved ciphers, the Z13 and the Z32. The deciphering process included the search for repeated patterns which could indicate how a cipher was constructed, but the two codes did not contain enough symbols to form many patterns. "They are very short, so even if someone stumbled on the right answers, there's no test to confirm them (unlike for Z408 and Z340)," Oranchak explained, "It's because so many plausible and reasonable solutions can be produced for both Z13 and Z32." Any proposed solution could seem correct, but the short ciphers made confirmation virtually impossible. In the absence of another stunning breakthrough in cryptographic ingenuity or answers from the killer himself, the secrets hidden in the Zodiac's other ciphers would most likely remain unknown.

The Z340 solution unlocked a cage and released the killer into the future. After almost half a century of silence, the Zodiac reached out from the past to haunt the world one more time. He hoped everyone was having fun trying to catch him and boasted that he was not afraid of death because his victims would serve him in eternity. The revelation of his message served as a stark reminder that the man who terrorized the citizens of the Bay Area was never caught. In 1969, he wrote, "The police shall never catch me, because I have been too clever for them." Those words may have sounded like a typical taunt back then, but now resonated as prophecy of the sad reality today. Dead or alive, the Zodiac had the last word.

Unsolved mysteries

Popular theories offered various explanations regarding the fate of the Zodiac. Speculation that he was either dead or in prison was often based on the assumption that the killer would still communicate if he was still alive and free. Yet other serial killers had been dormant as they married, had children, worked regular jobs, and avoided detection. Dennis Rader, aka "The B.T.K. Strangler," was the president of his church when he was arrested after eluding authorities for years. Rader was finally captured because he sent a computer disc that police were able to trace back to him. If the Zodiac was still alive, he probably knew any attempt to communicate with the media or police could lead to his arrest.

As time passed, the possibility that the Zodiac could still be alive was increasingly unlikely. He may have died without leaving behind any traces of his secret identity, such as the rest of Paul Stine's bloodstained shirt, the knife and guns used in the murders, or the hooded costume worn by the killer at Lake Berryessa. He might be identified by DNA found on an envelope or under a stamp, but that evidence might not be sufficient to prosecute a suspect in court and even a confession would require corroboration. DNA from Zodiac letters might identify a dead man, but police could be reluctant to officially close the case without direct evidence linking him to the crimes and therefore choose not to reveal his name to the public.

The hunt for the Zodiac continued as amateur sleuths accused new suspects and investigators turned to modern science with hopes of exposing the killer. Documentaries, books, podcasts, and websites kept the cold case in the spotlight, while other mysteries were largely forgotten chapters in true crime history. No one was ever charged for the murders of several female hitchhikers in Santa Rosa, California. The person who shot and killed Oceanside cabdriver, Ray Davis, in 1962 was never caught. Johnny Ray Swindle, his wife Joyce Ann, John Franklin Hood, and his fiancée Sandra Garcia were killed in seemingly random sniper attacks, but no suspects were ever arrested. The man who murdered Linda Edwards and Robert Domingos on a beach in 1963 was never captured. The murder of Cheri Jo Bates was still unsolved, and the disappearance and death of Donna Lass remained unexplained. Some theories attributed these and many other crimes to the Zodiac, although no one knew the true extent of the tragedy and horror left in his wake. As he wrote in one letter, "The task of filling up the blanks I rather leave up to you."

Decades ago, the legend of the Zodiac was created by destroying human beings who became his slaves in the afterlife, and their deaths were the foundation of his infamy. Without the victims, he was just another letter to the editor. Only time will tell if the killer is ever identified and justice is delivered for Paul Stine, Bryan Hartnell, Cecelia Shepard, Darlene Ferrin, Michael Mageau, David Faraday, and Betty Lou Jensen.

SOURCES:

Information about the crimes, the investigation, the suspects, and other aspects of the case was obtained from a variety of sources, including police reports, crime scene photographs, newspaper and magazine articles, television and radio broadcasts, books, internet sites, interviews conducted by the author, and official documents produced by the FBI, the Vallejo Police Department, the Benicia Police Department, the Sonoma County Sheriff's Office, the Napa County Sheriff's Office, the Napa Police Department, the San Francisco Police Department, the California Department of Justice, the Los Angeles Police Department, the Riverside Police Department, and more.

Index

Picture credits

Alamy: 42 (x2), 49, 54, 64, 110, 142, 147

Getty Images: 10, 22, 73, 75, 106

Public Domain: 13, 14, 27, 33, 44, 69, 76, 129, 185, 233

Shutterstock: 43

Wikimedia Commons: 114, 135, 189, 235